The Anatomy of K–12 Online Programs

The Anatomy of K–12 Online Programs

Practical Ideas and Guidelines

Doug Barnard and Jennifer Echols

ROWMAN & LITTLEFIELD
Lanham • Boulder • New York • London

Published by Rowman & Littlefield
A wholly owned subsidiary of The Rowman & Littlefield Publishing Group, Inc.
4501 Forbes Boulevard, Suite 200, Lanham, Maryland 20706
www.rowman.com

Unit A, Whitacre Mews, 26-34 Stannary Street, London SE11 4AB

Copyright © 2015 by Doug Barnard and Jennifer Echols

All rights reserved. No part of this book may be reproduced in any form or by any electronic or mechanical means, including information storage and retrieval systems, without written permission from the publisher, except by a reviewer who may quote passages in a review.

British Library Cataloguing in Publication Information Available

Library of Congress Cataloging-in-Publication Data

Barnard, Douglas P.
 The anatomy of K–12 online programs : practical ideas and guidelines / Doug Barnard and Jennifer Echols.
   pages cm
 Includes bibliographical references and index.
 ISBN 978-1-4758-0981-7 (cloth) — ISBN 978-1-4758-0982-4 (pbk.) — ISBN 978-1-4758-0983-1 (electronic) 1. Computer-assisted instruction—United States. 2. Internet in education—United States. 3. Web-based instruction—United States. 4. Education, Elementary—United States. 5. Education, Secondary—United States. I. Echols, Jennifer, 1969– II. Title.

LB1028.5.B296 2015
371.33'4—dc23   2014029857

Contents

List of Figures, Tables, and Textboxes		vii
Preface		ix
Acknowledgments		xi
Introduction		xiii
1	The Current Online Environment	1
2	Starting an Online Program	13
3	Curriculum	27
4	The Potential Impact of the Common Core	37
5	Academic Integrity	47
6	Evaluating Online Teachers and Specialists	59
7	Technology, Monitoring, and Functions	77
8	Future Trends and Issues	89
Appendix A		99
Bibliography		103
About the Authors		107

List of Figures, Tables, and Textboxes

Figure 2.1	14
Figure 2.2	15
Textbox 2.1	16
Figure 3.1	30
Figure 5.1	54
Figure 6.1	61
Figure 6.2	62
Figure 6.3	64
Figure 6.4	65
Figure 6.5	65
Figure 6.6	66
Figure 6.7	66
Figure 6.8	67
Table 6.1	68
Figure 7.1	83
Figure 7.2	84
Table A.1	100

Preface

This book was written by educators who spent fourteen years designing and developing an online program in the Mesa Public Schools (MPS) in Mesa, Arizona. MPS is the largest public school system in the state and one of first school districts to offer online courses in Arizona. The online program of MPS, the Mesa Distance Learning Program (MDLP), currently has partnerships with over thirty other school districts, supporting districts as needed in their mission to offer quality online courses.

Much like the human body, an online program is made up of various subsystems. Demonstrating how all of these systems work together efficiently as a whole is the purpose of this book and the reason for the title, *The Anatomy of K–12 Online Programs*. Appropriate monitoring of these subsystems is critical to the establishment of the improvement ethic: a core belief that allows a program to focus on academic excellence and be sustainable over time.

The goal of the authors was to present reality—blemishes and all—of the inner workings of a school district program. It is intended to serve as a guide for school districts and also as a college text for educators who want to learn more about online learning in the real world. The intent is to provide an overview of practices and models for other educators who are attempting to solve problems or develop their own online program. This book is not meant to offer the one and only solution to any single problem, but rather to share the authors' experience in public K–12 school districts, with the hope of assisting other districts as they decide what is best for their unique situation.

Acknowledgments

This book would never have been written without the leadership of several superintendents of the Mesa Public Schools. Dr. James Zaharis was the superintendent when the idea for the Mesa Distance Learning Program (MDLP) was conceived, and his leadership allowed the idea to begin development in 1999. After Dr. Zaharis retired, Dr. Debra Duvall encouraged the refinements that allowed the MDLP to become the largest program in Arizona and the second largest in the country. Dr. Mike Cowan took the helm after Dr. Duvall retired, and as superintendent, has given his full support to MDLP. Dr. Cowan also gave permission to use the ideas and processes used in the MDLP program as part of this book.

The MDLP staff deserves credit for developing ideas and persevering in their refinement to ensure the program is the best it can be. The certified and classified staff had a huge part in developing the reputation of the MDLP program. The content specialists who developed the processes used in the program were committed to the goal of providing support to one another and to the clients we served. The staff lived the improvement ethic every day.

A special "shout out" to Terry Hutchins—a unique combination of educator and programmer with the talent to create the MDLP management system, the heart and soul of the Mesa Distance Learning Program. When an idea was presented to the staff, the task of programming was handed to Terry, who always came up with a better plan than the rest of us had in the beginning. Terry is affectionately known as the "resident genius" and still is very involved with the Mesa Distance Learning Program.

Last, but most important, we thank our families for being patient with us and supporting us in writing this book. We couldn't have written this book without all the people mentioned in these acknowledgments.

Introduction

The book is designed so that readers can skip around and find ideas to help develop new programs, improve existing programs, and resolve issues they are facing.

1. Chapter 1: The goal in this chapter is to define the current online environment, including common myths, essential program components, and the many challenges facing online programs. It also discusses the lack of oversight and the politics that impact online learning.
2. Chapter 2: This chapter describes the critical attributes of an online program, including key decisions and the importance of defining the vision, mission, and core beliefs. It explains all components needed to have a quality program: teachers, training, accreditation, and the selection of technology.
3. Chapter 3: This chapter gets at the nitty-gritty of the curriculum and alignment to the state standards. It provides a clear explanation as to how selection of the curriculum relates to the overall program structure. This chapter provides an overview of critical components in online content: chunking, frequent feedback, student engagement, and a universal design for learning.
4. Chapter 4: This chapter tackles the issue of using the Common Core in an online setting, including the impact on lesson design, high-stakes testing, the cost, and training of online teachers. The history of previous accountability efforts and the future of the Common Core are also discussed.

5. Chapter 5: Many of the concerns with online learning are related to the issue of academic integrity, and an entire chapter is devoted to the topic. Key concepts related to academic honesty and misconduct are presented: requiring proctored final exams, how students cheat in the online environment, appropriate consequences, and suggestions for preventing and mitigating academic misconduct.
6. Chapter 6: What evidence can be used by online programs to evaluate online teachers? Ideas and methods for effective online evaluation systems are presented in detail.
7. Chapter 7: The learning management system (LMS) is the backbone of an online program, and helps determine how a program functions on a daily basis. This chapter discusses the functions of the LMS and how an effective LMS is used to monitor the subsystems within the program.
8. Chapter 8: Where are online programs headed? This chapter discusses key issues that will determine the future impact of the online movement.

CHAPTER 1

The Current Online Environment

There are about fifty million K–12 students in the United States, but nobody really knows how many of these students are enrolled in online learning programs.[1] Accurate records for online course enrollments are not kept by all states, so any number is at best an estimate. The International Association for K–12 Online Learning (iNACOL) surveyed individual school districts across the nation and reported, "The total number of students taking part in all of these programs is unknown, but is likely several million, or slightly more than 5 percent of the total K–12 student population across the United States."[2] This chapter will provide an overview of the current state of K–12 online learning in the United States, including its explosive growth and challenges that must be addressed to ensure the sustainability of online learning.

INCREASING ENROLLMENT IN K–12 ONLINE PROGRAMS

Although accurate numbers are unavailable, it is safe to say that K–12 enrollment in online courses is increasing. The Mesa Distance Learning Program (MDLP), the online program developed by the Mesa Public Schools in Mesa, Arizona, is an example of the dramatic increase in online enrollment. More students are enrolled in fully online programs in Arizona than in any other state. The percentage of Arizona's K–12 fully online population is 4.28 percent, significantly higher than in any other state.[3] Despite the growth in the number of K–12 students taking online courses in Arizona and other states, the overall number of students taking online courses across the nation is relatively low; online learning is still in its infancy. All stakeholders, including educators and commercial vendors, offer a variety of prophecies as to how online programs will mature and be sustainable within the public school systems in all states.

A common perception of students and parents is that all K–12 online programs are essentially the same. Nothing could be further from the truth! The proliferation of schools using commercial online programs has created a competitive atmosphere—among online providers attempting to attract revenue, and among schools attempting to attract students. The rapid growth of online schools and products can be confusing for school districts, parents, and students who are trying to determine which option is best.

The explosive growth of online learning is driven by three factors: politics, money, and technological innovations. Arizona is an excellent example of how these factors have intersected to create a variety of online educational options for families. One has to wonder how a small state in terms of population like Arizona can have more online students than California or any other state with a larger population. The reason for this proliferation is the conservative political atmosphere in the Arizona state legislature, which favors the idea that private enterprise is better able to produce meaningful educational reform than a government agency. Over the years, legislation has allowed enterprising entrepreneurs to change education in Arizona.

Online learning at the K–12 level officially began in Arizona in 1999 when a state law authorized a pilot program for two charter and two public school programs. Lobbyists quickly forced the expansion of the pilot to fourteen—seven charter and seven public school programs. After additional pressure from lobbyists, in 2009, the legislature passed a bill allowing any school district or charter school to become an authorized online provider simply by filling out a proposal form and submitting it for approval to the Arizona Department of Education. As of July 2013, there were seventy-four online programs operating in Arizona.[4]

COMMON MYTHS ABOUT ONLINE LEARNING

An example of the explosion of online education can be seen by turning on the television. Frequent viewers of programming geared to families have likely seen a commercial advertising the merits of a free public online school. These commercials typically portray a child or young adult flourishing in the online school environment. The smiling student is shown sitting at the computer, with a parent close by to help and monitor the student's progress. The message of the commercial is clear: although the traditional public school failed this student, the online school is meeting all of the student's individual needs while delivering a rigorous yet engaging curriculum. This ideal situation looks good on television, but like much of what is seen on TV, it is not reality.

There is a place for online learning within the K–12 educational system, but it is not a cure-all—or even a good match for every student. Districts and individual schools must carefully consider the demographics of their community and their mission to determine why, how, and when online learning is a viable option. Unfortunately, many districts and schools jump into online learning having given little thought to how an online program will meet the needs of students. The result often leaves schools tied to expensive subscriptions with for-profit curriculum vendors, and dealing with complaints from frustrated teachers, parents, and students.

ESSENTIAL PROGRAM COMPONENTS

A "one size fits all" online program does not exist. In the K–12 online world, programs vary in large and small ways—starting with their basic purpose (commercial, for-profit vs. educational, non-profit), to the method of delivery (synchronous vs. asynchronous, computer-based or teacher-led instruction), to the quality and rigor of the curriculum. There are, however, some elements that should be present in any program to ensure that it will serve the best interests of students, parents, and schools.

1. The curriculum should be based on local and state standards.
2. The curriculum should be delivered in a manner that demands student engagement.
3. Critical thinking skills should be taught, practiced, and assessed.
4. The program should employ procedures to maintain academic integrity.

5. Students should have access to a highly qualified teacher who provides frequent feedback about their learning.
6. The program should be able to produce evidence of learning.

CHALLENGES FACING ONLINE PROGRAMS

There has been much debate over the role of online learning in K–12 education. Some proponents insist that it is the technological innovation with the ability to revolutionize education by personalizing learning. Critics contend that online courses are being used as an inexpensive way to replace teachers, yet no credible evidence exists to support that online learning is as effective for K–12 learners as face-to-face instruction. Both sides agree, however, that major issues have been raised and will continue to impact the outcome for K–12 online learning.

1. *Academic integrity*: It is a common perception that online students regularly and willfully engage in academic misconduct, but the practice is ignored or even tacitly accepted by some programs. Until online programs can give assurances to others that students are completing their own course work, and provide evidence of mastery of key concepts and skills, they will always lack credibility with other educational institutions. Although the academic integrity policy is at the heart of a quality online program, for-profit programs are resistant to the implementation of academic integrity procedures because they require continual monitoring—measures that can be costly. For example, in Arizona, lobbyists worked zealously to successfully prevent the passage of a law that would have required the proctoring of final exams by a qualified school official. Chapter 5 will address the issue of academic integrity in greater detail.
2. *Transparency of teacher qualifications*: Some programs use non-certified personnel to teach courses. This criticism is directed at charter schools, since most states do not require charter schools to hire certificated staff. Criticism has also been levied against nationwide commercial programs for outsourcing instructional work to laborers outside of the United States. Although most programs do not outsource grading, and the outsource of grad-

ing is not illegal, the practice casts online programs in a negative light. Parents and students understand that state-mandated, high-stakes tests are not locally scored, but expect that course work will be evaluated and feedback provided by a local teacher. Some commercial schools and programs claim that courses are taught by certified teachers, but these certified teachers only supervise advisers or facilitators (who lack certification or other qualifications) and interact with students. Online programs should be upfront regarding the qualifications and location of teachers and other staff who will work with students.

3. *Acceptance of credits by the National Collegiate Athletic Association (NCAA) and the military*: The NCAA and military recruiters do not automatically accept credits from online institutions, even if the programs are accredited. A lack of rigor and academic integrity are reasons that credits are not always accepted by other institutions. It is important for school districts, parents, and students to carefully vet programs before choosing an online provider.

4. *High dropout rate*: Online programs at all levels, including the collegiate level, suffer from higher dropout rates than brick-and-mortar schools. A 2011 analysis of full-time online education programs in Colorado demonstrates the extent of the problem: "The dropout rate in the top 10 largest online programs last year was 12 percent—quadruple the state average of 3 percent. Colorado's online schools produced three times more dropouts than graduates. That's the opposite of the state average, where there are three graduates for every one dropout."[5] Although these numbers are specific to Colorado, online schools and programs across the nation also suffer from high dropout rates. Online programs need to identify the root causes of the dropout problem and find ways to address the issue.

5. *Many schools use online programs as "dumping grounds" for students who have not been successful in a traditional environment*: Credit recovery is one of the fastest-growing segments of online learning. Although the intent is worthy, it might not be the best place for this type of student to learn. Experience has shown that if a student is upside down in a traditional setting, he or she

will flounder in the online environment without adequate supervision and access to support systems like tutoring. The improper use of online learning for credit recovery is one reason for the high dropout rate.
6. *Serving students with special needs in the online environment*: To comply with Section 504 of the Rehabilitation Act and Title II of the Americans with Disabilities Act, online programs must provide equal access to educational opportunities. This has implications for program structure and course design. The online setting may not be the best educational environment for every student, but the school should be prepared to offer a better option before turning a student away. Considerations for choosing or creating accessible curriculum will be discussed in Chapter 3.
7. *Maintaining program efficiency*: School districts need to be good stewards of public funds, but developing and deploying an online program can be an expensive endeavor. There are efficient ways to offer quality online learning in a sustainable manner, such as providing courses through a program with a proven track record. School districts should consider both commercial products as well as options offered by other school districts. For example, after the Mesa Distance Learning Program started in 1999, it became a model for other school districts. MDLP took the position of being a good neighbor and helping other school districts by providing courses to students in other districts through intergovernmental agreements or by providing guidance to districts as they developed their own programs. Currently, there are about thirty school districts in Arizona that offer online courses to their students through the Mesa Distance Learning Program. MDLP allows partner districts to offer high-quality courses and academic integrity in a cost-efficient manner.
8. *Evaluation of online programs*: The use of standardized test scores is not the best means to evaluate online programs and schools, as the full-time population is transient and a majority of these students are focused on credit recovery. Online programs tend to have significant numbers of students who take most of their courses in a traditional setting and only a few courses online. Although the achievement for these part-time students should be

included in aggregate data on school report cards, state systems are often unable to attribute test scores to more than one institution. Therefore, achievement data reported for online schools and programs are culled from a narrow part of the population, resulting in inaccurate labels. A consistent and valid method of evaluation would allow students, parents, and schools to choose an online provider that teaches students skills that will allow them to be successful at the next level of learning.

9. *Alignment to state standards*: Schools that lack the personnel and technological resources to develop their own online programs from the ground up often turn to commercial programs to provide curriculum and other elements of the online environment. Commercial vendors build curriculum for a nationwide audience, and connect it to individual state standards after the fact. The end result is curriculum that may not be closely aligned to state and local standards. Whether curriculum is developed in-house by district personnel or purchased from a commercial vendor, it is a challenge to maintain alignment to changes in state and local standards.

THE OVERSIGHT OF ONLINE PROGRAMS

The challenges faced by online programs ought to be addressed at a state level to ensure an equitable solution for schools and students. However, state departments of education have found it difficult to monitor online programs, as demonstrated in Arizona and Minnesota. In Arizona, the auditor general has conducted only one audit of online programs since the inception of K–12 online learning in 1999. The 2006 audit reviewed seven public school programs and seven charter school programs. The audit report, released in 2007, identified violations and areas for improvement, and recommended specific corrections. Although some of the problems were fixed, some of the issues have never been corrected. In the annual report to the state board of education, the Arizona Department of Education blamed a lack of resources for the failure to address all of the issues identified in the audit's report.[6] A more recent audit of online learning was conducted in Minnesota in 2010. The 2011 report released by the Minnesota Office of the Legislative Auditor revealed that lack of oversight was also a problem in that state: "A large part of the department's oversight problems are due to the fact that the Minnesota Department of Education has not assigned sufficient staff to fulfill its online learning responsibilities since mid-2009."[7]

Even if states had adequate personnel to monitor online programs, appropriate methods for collecting data regarding student achievement have not been developed by state education departments. The data collection methods used to monitor traditional brick-and-mortar schools are not appropriate for online programs, yet these measures are still applied. The Minnesota audit report recognized this problem: "Minnesota Department of Education data regarding online learning do not present a complete and accurate picture of online learning in Minnesota."[8] In Arizona, the state system for tracking student achievement is not capable of attributing achievement data to multiple institutions. Most students (90 percent in Mesa Public Schools) who take online courses are concurrently enrolled at a brick-and-mortar school, but online programs only receive data for full-time students. Therefore, the achievement data provided for online programs are highly inaccurate.

The quality of online learning would be greatly improved if each state provided adequate resources to create appropriate oversight procedures and the personnel to properly implement those procedures. The state should maintain a database of the online programs available to schools and students, including information about the structure and format of classes, course completion rates, level of difficulty, and student achievement statistics. This would provide parents with a system that conveys which program produces the best results. It would be appropriate for each state to have a state-sponsored and -funded program, open to any school or student in the state. A quality state program would provide equal access to all students and address the inequity issues faced by small, rural, or impoverished districts. There are twenty-seven state programs out of the fifty states, leaving twenty-three states without a statewide program option.

THE POLITICS OF ONLINE LEARNING

It is a reality of life that politics are played anytime more than two people are involved in any situation. The role of politics in education is evident at the local, state, and national levels; the current fight over the adoption and implementation of the Common Core standards is just one example. Politics are usually involved in education as individuals and groups fight for control, but in the world of online learning, politics are driven by money. It is important for parents, educators, and administrators to be aware of the politics of K–12 online learning and make their own voices heard. Online learning in K–12 schools will be successful only if stakeholders in the trenches become advocates for best practices.

K–12 online learning presents opportunities for businesses and individuals to make money. School districts generally do not have the resources at their disposal to develop online courses in-house, so they look to vendors for curriculum, learning management systems, and other technologies. These vendors want to ensure that school districts have continued access to their products, so they hire lobbyists to influence legislation at the state and national levels. The opportunity to profit is even greater in states like Arizona that allow for-profit charter schools to operate.

Lobbyists have influenced and will continue to influence legislation that determines how online programs operate in each state. Therefore, it is imperative that online administrators monitor the legislative process for bills that impact online learning and share their concerns with legislators. Larger school districts may employ their own lobbyists or have other connections at the state level. Any constituent can reach out to his or her legislator through phone calls or e-mails, so online administrators should keep their communities informed about bills related to online learning. Representatives from online programs should request to speak to legislative committees regarding proposed legislation to share the potential impact of the bill on online programs and/or suggest alternative wording. There are four critical areas to be monitored in terms of online learning legislation: digital choice, funding, teacher certification, and academic integrity.

- *Digital choice*: In this context, the term "digital choice" is being used to refer to state policies and laws that allow students to take courses from any approved online provider. The digital choice concept is good in theory, because it provides access to online courses to students throughout the state. However, digital choice laws may not include standards for course quality, rigor, or academic integrity. Ideally, state laws regarding online learning should provide mechanisms for monitoring course quality and challenging online providers who offer insufficient or inappropriate curriculum.

If the quality of online courses is not properly monitored, digital choice laws can have a negative impact on student learning and achievement. For example, in Arizona, several for-profit charter schools are well known to students for offering free courses that lack rigor. Students who are deficient in credits often take courses through one of these online schools in lieu of credit recovery options in their home school districts. School districts, concerned about accepting transfer credits from a substandard institution, refused to allow credits taken from certain online institutions. Lobbyists working on behalf of the for-profit online charter schools got involved, and secured the passage of legislation that restricted the ability of a school district to refuse the credits.

The concept of digital choice already exists or is being pushed in many states. Digital choice allows students to take an online course from an approved provider at no out-of-pocket cost to the student. The course cost is passed on to the student's home school district by diverting some of the per-pupil funding to the digital course provider. Advocates claim digital choice benefits students by allowing them to take courses that best suit their needs and interests. However, already cash-strapped brick-and-mortar schools will struggle to meet the needs of students in the face-to-face setting if adjustments are not made to the funding model.

- *Funding*: The method of funding online schools and programs varies by state, but it is generally not the same funding model used for brick-and-mortar schools. Most states only allow a certain amount of funding per pupil, so allowing students to choose an online provider outside of the school district may negatively impact the amount of funding received, even though the level of service provided by the district has not decreased.

  Lobbyists have been active in state legislatures pushing for a variety of creative funding methods. A common element in many of the funding models is withholding at least some of the funding until the course is completed. *Keeping Pace* explains: "In Louisiana and Utah, 50% of a course fee is paid upon student enrollment, and 50% is paid upon timely completion (providers may receive 40% if a student eventually completes and receives credit for the course). In Michigan, a district pays 80% upon enrollment and 20% upon completion."[9] Other states, like Florida and Minnesota, require course completion for any funding to be generated.

There are concerns related to funding based upon course completion. The high dropout rate for online programs means that funding models like Michigan's have the potential for online course providers (often for-profit institutions) to collect a substantial amount of funding while providing minimal services. However, there is another side to this argument; funding models that require course completion may encourage the use of unethical methods to prompt students to complete a course. Perhaps the best funding model would be one that combines course completion with a performance-based assessment that demonstrates student mastery for full funding to be generated.

SUMMARY

Online learning at the K–12 level is at a crossroads; while the innovation holds much promise, it also faces major challenges in terms of funding, credibility, and accountability. The road taken as a distance learning community—including charter, private, and district schools—will either yield greater respect for online learning as a viable option for K–12 students by ensuring program creditability, academic integrity, and accountability, or provide further evidence that some programs operate only for the almighty dollar. The problems of too much politics and not enough oversight need to be remedied to build greater accountability and credibility for online learning.

NOTES

1. United States Census Bureau, "The 2012 Statistical Abstract, Education," Elementary and Secondary Education, Schools Enrollment Table 243,

accessed October 9, 2013, https://www.census.gov/compendia/statab/cats/education.html.

2. Butch Gemin et al., *Keeping Pace with K–12 Online and Blended Learning: An Annual Review of Policy and Practice* (Evergreen Education Group, 2012): 4, http://kpk12.com/cms/wp-content/uploads/KeepingPace2012.pdf.

3. Ibid., 23.

4. Ibid., 14.

5. Burt Hubbard and Nancy Mitchell, "Achievement of Online Students Drops over Time, Lags State Averages on Every Indicator," Chalkbeat Colorado, October 3, 2011, accessed October 1, 2013, http://co.chalkbeat.org/2011/10/03/achievement-of-online-students-drops-over-time-lags-state-wide-averages-on-every-indicator/.

6. State of Arizona Office of the Auditor General, "Technology Assisted Project-Based Instruction Program: Auditor General Performance Audit Report 4th Follow-Up Report," accessed October 1, 2013, http://www.azauditor.gov/Reports/School_Districts/Statewide/tapbi/Oct07/TAPBI_4thFollowup.pdf.

7. Office of the Legislative Auditor State of Minnesota, "Evaluation Report: K–12 Online Learning," accessed October 1, 2013, http://www.auditor.leg.state.mn.us/ped/pedrep/k12oll.pdf.

8. Ibid.

9. Gemin et al., *Keeping Pace*, 36.

CHAPTER 2

Starting an Online Program

Consider the automobile—it is available in a variety of configurations, but the basic components are the same. Every car or truck has a body, an engine, and a transmission, but the quality and performance of these components greatly influence the cost and functionality of the automobile. This analogy can be applied to online programs; although all programs have the same basic components, the overall quality, function, and size of the programs can be vastly different.

A comprehensive online program will have seven elements that have a significant impact on student learning. As the graphic illustrates, the learning management system (LMS) is the backbone that connects and supports all other program components.

School districts interested in building an online program often start the process by sending out a request for proposal (RFP) to allow commercial companies and other educational institutions to make presentations. As noted in Chapter 1, this unfortunate approach causes districts to dive into the "how" part of online learning by selecting the technology before determining reasons for the program and the needs it will fulfill. The success of an online program depends upon being built on a strong foundation of a clearly defined vision, mission, and core beliefs. The graphic below shows a suggested process for the development of an online program.

DEFINE THE VISION, MISSION, AND CORE BELIEFS

The vision is the first building block of a quality online program. A Japanese proverb shows the importance of vision: "Vision without ac-

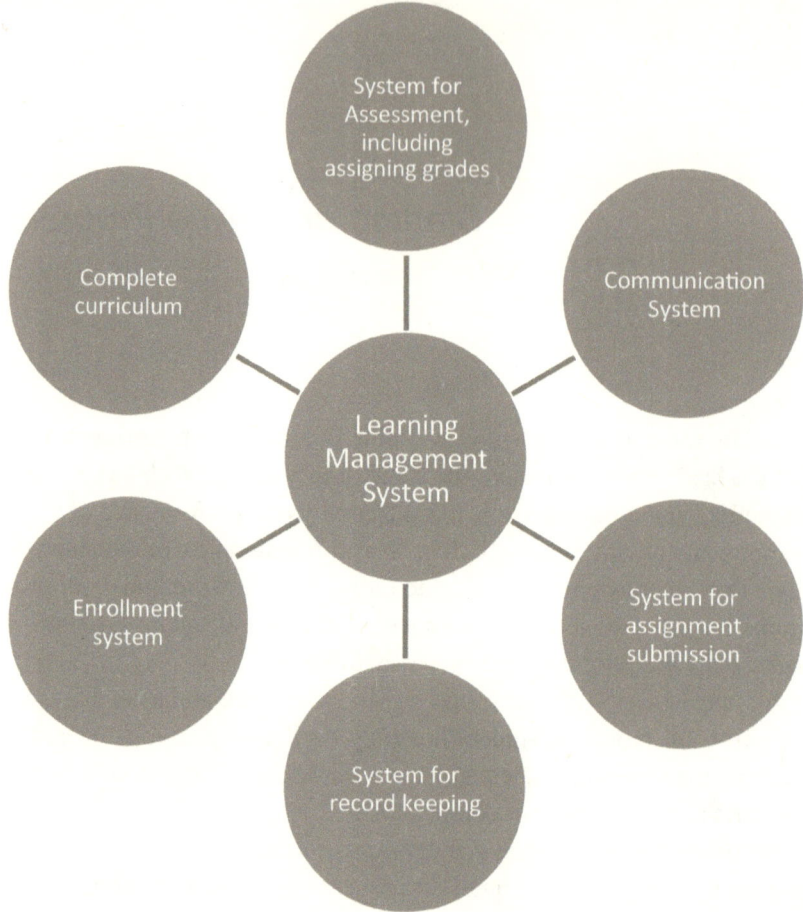

Figure 2.1.

tion is a daydream. Action without vision is a nightmare." The school district leadership should articulate what the program will look like and how it will function when it is fully developed. Once the vision is articulated, a committee can be formed to determine the development process. The composition of this committee deserves careful consideration. Stakeholders representing the groups who will be most impacted by the program should be included, but avoid creating a committee that is too large; a larger committee lengthens every task and prolongs the

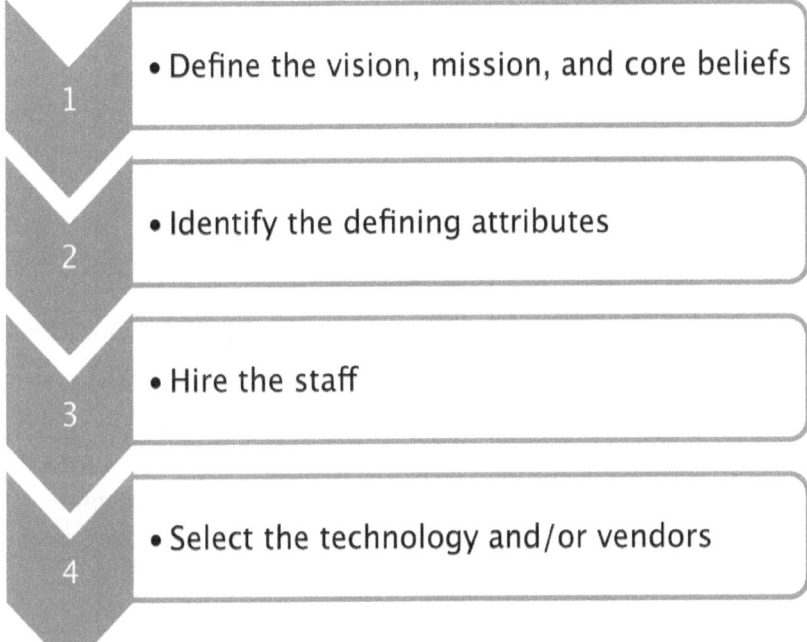

Figure 2.2.

entire process. An important role for committee members will be to carry the message about the program back to the groups they represent and help create buy-in throughout the district. The composition of the committee will determine outcome for the project.

Once the committee is formed, the hard work begins. The first step in the development process is articulating a mission statement that encompasses the reasons for the program. Listed below is the initial mission statement of the Mesa Distance Learning Program (MDLP).

Vision and mission statements grow out of core beliefs. The core beliefs should be communicated to stakeholders, including parents, administrators, and teachers, to ensure they understand that the program is being developed to meet the needs of students. In particular, administrators and teachers may need reassurance that the program is not designed to take students from their schools, but rather to provide options to maximize student achievement. MDLP was founded upon

> **TEXTBOX 2.1**
> **MESA DISTANCE LEARNING PROGRAM (MDLP)**
>
> **MISSION STATEMENT**
>
> The primary mission of the Mesa Distance Learning Program is to develop and provide high-quality online education for K–12 students that aligns with district, state, and national academic standards. Since distance learning is changing rapidly, MDLP will utilize "improvement ethic" processes by incorporating new research from technology and teaching strategies into our program. The Mesa Distance Learning Program strives to meet the varying needs of students and families by allowing them the option of using the program as a supplement to traditional schooling or continuing with the program full-time to earn a high school diploma.

two core beliefs that were communicated anytime the program was presented to a group of educators or community members:

1. The best place for a student to learn is in the classroom, interacting with the teacher and other students in the class.
2. If this setting is not possible due to health or other reasons, then online learning can be a viable option.

IDENTIFY THE DEFINING ATTRIBUTES

The next step in the process involves developing a comprehensive picture of what the program will look like and how it will function. The use of defining questions is suggested to help focus the discussion on the desired attributes, develop a preliminary budget, and identify equipment and space needs. The identification of desired attributes that align with the vision, mission, and core beliefs makes it easy to select the appropriate technology to implement the program. Bypassing this critical step often leads to the selection of a learning management system and/or curriculum that does not meet the particular needs of a school district.

Suggested Defining Questions

Appendix A contains a list of the defining questions explained in detail below. This appendix can be used by each committee member to make notes during the discussion. The form includes a place for the estimated cost for each component to assist in the development of a preliminary budget.

1. *Who will be served by the program?*
   a. *Grade levels*: A program might serve students at one level (elementary, middle, or high school) or it might serve students at all levels K–12. A conservative approach is to start by serving students at one level, adding other grade levels over time as dictated by program growth and student needs. MDLP started by offering courses to high school students, next adding grades seven and eight, and eventually elementary courses.
   b. *Academic levels*: There are significant differences in terms of structure, readability, and rigor among online courses designed for credit recovery, regular track, and honors/gifted/advanced placement track. Again, it may be wise to start a program with course offerings in one area and expand to other tracks as needed.
   c. *Enrollment status*: Will the program serve full-time students who take all of their classes online, part-time students who use the program as a supplement to traditional school, or both? State funding is generally tied to a student's enrollment status, with more funding available for full-time students. However, a majority of students enrolled in online courses at the high school level use it as a supplement to the traditional school.
2. *What method will be used for program delivery?*
   a. *Synchronous delivery*: This method of delivery means that students are enrolled in a cohort with a defined start and end

date. There are several advantages to synchronous delivery, including allowing for student-to-student interaction through collaborative assignments and real-time discussion. Teachers can identify subgroups who need remediation and arrange for small-group tutoring sessions. Disadvantages of this approach include the loss of flexibility in terms of enrollment and the management of teacher loads. The dropout rate for online courses is significantly higher than for a traditional classroom, so a teacher who starts with thirty students may have significantly fewer students by the end of the semester.
   b. *Asynchronous delivery*: This method of delivery is more flexible because it allows for open-entry enrollment, and also makes it easy to balance teacher loads. However, the asynchronous environment is not conducive to student-to-student collaboration, which is an important component of the Common Core.
   c. *Blended model*: According to the Christensen Institute, the definition of blended learning is "a formal education program in which a student learns at least in part through online learning, with some element of student control over time, place, path, and/or pace; at least in part in a supervised brick-and-mortar location away from home; and the modalities along each student's learning path within a course or subject are connected to provide an integrated learning experience."[1] The blended model can be used in a synchronous or asynchronous format.
3. *Single-district or multi-district program?* A single-district program serves students residing within one district, while a multi-district program serves students in multiple districts. Serving students from multiple districts requires a larger staff and a higher level of expertise.
4. *Will curriculum be purchased from a vendor or developed in-house?*
   a. *Curriculum vendors*: There are many options available to K–12 schools in terms of online curriculum. Using curriculum developed by a vendor may expedite the program develop-

ment timeline and provide access to features that school districts lack the expertise to develop on their own. Commercial curriculum products are typically developed to be used by schools throughout the nation, so they may lack specific alignment to district or state standards. Cost is another important consideration for purchasing curriculum, as there is often a start-up fee, training costs, and an ongoing subscription cost.

b. *Open-source curriculum*: The use of open-source curriculum is becoming increasingly prevalent in online learning. According to the William and Flora Hewlett Foundation, open educational resources (OER) "are teaching, learning, and research resources that reside in the public domain or have been released under an intellectual property license that permits their free use and re-purposing by others. Open educational resources include full courses, course materials, modules, textbooks, streaming videos, tests, software, and any other tools, materials, or techniques used to support access to knowledge."[2] The use of OER is attractive to many schools because the resources are free for non-commercial users, and the quality of some of the resources is very high. However, these resources are developed for a global audience, so they require careful vetting to ensure that they are aligned to specific state and local standards and are appropriate for the ability and age levels of the students to be served.

c. *In-house course development*: Developing courses in-house requires the appropriate technology and the right staff—content area experts and developers with knowledge of the K–12 online environment and expertise using technology. When courses are developed in-house, alignment with district and state standards can be ensured, and modifications can be made as needed. In the long run, this approach is less expensive than using commercial curriculum, but it does require a significant initial investment.

At this point in the process, it is only being determined if curriculum will be purchased or developed; it is not yet time to select specific vendors or hire developers. It is essential to have a clear

picture of how the program will look and function before technology or staff are identified.
5. *What learning management system will be used?* The LMS should demonstrate the ability to collect and store data, and generate reports as requested by parents or schools, such as log-in records, course activity logs, costs, course enrollments, and grade distribution. The LMS is the backbone of the online learning program, so it is important to choose a system that will meet the specific needs of the program.
    a. *Curriculum vendor-hosted systems*: Commercial vendors will likely provide an LMS and offer hosting services with their curriculum. These systems are generally referred to as closed systems, because they do not allow for customization of specific features.
    b. *Commercial systems*: Districts choosing to develop curriculum in-house will also need an LMS. Commercial LMS options, such as Blackboard, are available for a subscription fee. The benefit of using a commercial LMS is that minimal technical expertise is required. A commercial system may allow for some customization, but additional costs are likely to be associated with customization.
    c. *Open-source systems*: Open-source learning management systems, like Moodle, are a lower-cost option (often free) and allow users to customize some features, but require greater technical competence to be used effectively.
    d. *Proprietary systems*: A fourth option is to develop a proprietary LMS that is specific to the needs of the program. This option requires a programmer to build and maintain the system, but allows for the greatest flexibility and customization. When MDLP first began operating, a commercial LMS was used. It quickly became apparent that any third-party LMS was limited in its ability to customize specific features in a timely manner. The decision was made to invest in a full-time programmer to create and maintain a proprietary system, allowing the program to implement changes as needed and efficiently manage adherence to state reporting guidelines.

6. *How will communication be maintained among stakeholders?* The communication system should facilitate communication among all stakeholders: students, parents, online teachers, lab teachers, counselors, and administrators. A key feature for the communication system is the ability to send automated reports, such as student progress reports. Consider whether this feature is embedded in the LMS or if a separate system must be developed.
7. *How many courses will be offered when the program is launched?* The answer to this question may be dictated by the choice of curriculum. In-house curriculum development takes time, so districts following this path may need to start small with a few in-demand courses and add courses over time. Districts using commercial curriculum will have the option of launching the program with numerous course offerings, but there is wisdom in starting small so that problems can be identified and resolved before expanding.
8. *Where will students access online courses?* Many districts choose to offer students access to online courses in computer labs before, during, or after school hours. This model allows students to be served who do not have a computer or Internet access at home, and provides support for students who are not independent learners. When providing computer lab access, districts must consider space, equipment, and personnel requirements.
9. *How will the online program service students with special needs?* In the current online environment, there is a heightened focus on providing services to students with special needs. In particular, curriculum should be designed with accessibility in mind. Online programs should also have established procedures for communication among special education case managers, parents, and teachers to ensure that accommodations are being provided to students with individualized education programs (IEPs) and 504 plans.
10. *How will the program be hosted?* Districts must determine whether the program will be hosted in-house by the district information systems (IS) department, or hosted off-site. Subscriptions

to a commercial curriculum and/or LMS may include hosting services, but some systems will require the district to purchase and host its own server. It is important to choose the most reliable hosting service available, because learning stops when online courses are not available. School district IS departments are responsible for keeping all technology throughout the district operational and may not be able to make the online program a priority. If the decision is made to buy and host the server, consider using professional hosting services outside of the school district to ensure continuity of service.

11. *Who will teach online courses?* There are many important factors to consider when selecting teachers for the online program.
    a. *Will full-time or part-time teachers be used?* Full-time teachers can manage a higher student count and be available for weekly online office hours. Hiring full-time teachers is more costly than paying part-time teachers.
    b. *How will part-time teachers be paid?* Part-time teachers may be paid according to the student count, by a stipend, or hourly. Factors that influence this decision include a high dropout rate for K–12 online students, whether the program uses a cohort-based or open-entry model, and the amount of student-teacher interaction demanded by the curriculum.
    c. *How will teachers be supervised?* Expectations for online teachers should be developed, as well as a method for evaluation and a system for monitoring.
    d. *How will teachers be trained?* Teachers will need initial and ongoing training. Some training should be face-to-face, but on-demand training should be available for teachers working at different times and in different locations.

12. *What other staff will be required to launch the program?* The answer to this question will be dictated by the size and scope of the program, but at least some staff must be dedicated to the program full time. A common mistake in online program development is to assign oversight to an administrator who has other responsibilities in the district. An effective program will have a principal or director whose primary task is online learning. In

addition to the program administrator, specialists who can serve as content area experts and developers, a counselor (at least part-time), and a registrar will be needed to launch the program. At least one of the specialists should have the technical expertise to maintain the website or serve as the liaison to the web hosting provider. Other staff can be added as the program grows.

13. *How will student records be managed?* All school districts use software to manage student records and make reports to the state, and it must be determined whether the LMS for the online program will integrate with the district system. If not, a plan for tracking and reporting student attendance and achievement in adherence with state requirements must be developed.

14. *How will the online program be accredited?* Some online programs are accredited under the umbrella of district accreditation, but it may be necessary to obtain separate accreditation for the online school or program. Accreditation will determine whether the course credits will be accepted by universities, the military, other public schools, and the National Collegiate Athletic Association (NCAA).

15. *How will the program be marketed?* Develop a plan to inform the community when the program is ready to be launched. School staff (administrators, counselors, and teachers), parents, and students should be informed of the course offerings, procedures for enrolling, and deadlines.

16. *How will technical support be provided to users?* Effective online programs include a support network for technical issues and content-related questions. How will the support system work? Consider who will provide the support and the method of delivery—e-mail, phone, or both.

As the committee discusses the defining questions, a clear picture of the desired attributes, aligned to the vision and mission, should emerge. The committee should present the proposal to district and school administration members, curriculum specialists, and other stakeholders, seeking input and being open to feedback. Be sure to include a timeline in the proposal to avoid delays in launching the program.

HIRE THE STAFF

Perhaps the most important consideration when starting an online program is the selection of the program administrator, as this individual will provide the vision and grow the program. Essential qualifications for this position include a background in education, competence with educational technology, and expertise in curriculum development. The program administrator should be chosen first, because this person will need to select the other staff members.

The initial staff for any online program is generally small, making it essential for the director to select team members who are passionate about online learning and are the best fit for the job. As in any educational setting, team members will wear many hats, so it is important to choose people who are able to be flexible and multitask. Customer service skills are a must-have quality, because the program staff will deal with students, parents, administrators, counselors, and teachers. Most important, every team member should share the director's vision and embrace the program's philosophy.

Prior to hiring teachers, expectations and standards for online teachers should be clearly delineated. Many classroom teachers are interested in working in the online environment, either in a part- or full-time capacity. However, great classroom teaching does not always translate to great online teaching. Content knowledge, flexibility, written communication skills, and technical expertise are critical factors for successful online teachers. Great teachers are a critical element in student achievement, whether the classroom is in a brick-and-mortar building or online.

A key decision in the development of MDLP was to hire teachers from within the district, assuaging concerns that the online program was a way to replace classroom teachers. MDLP sought out teacher-leaders from within the Mesa Public Schools who were recognized for their content area and teaching expertise. Having the most qualified teachers on staff not only contributes to student achievement, but also sends a message to the community about the quality of the program.

AWARENESS OF CRITICS

District and program leadership needs to be aware of the different views of online learning that may be held by teachers, administrators, and parents. Leaders can prevent backlash against the program by being aware of potential criticisms:

1. Some administrators and teachers believe that online learning is a way to replace teachers or take students away from schools. The best way to combat this belief is by hiring teachers from within the district to teach online classes, and show administrators how online courses can benefit students and schools.
2. Students in the primary grades need to be working with a teacher rather than sitting in front of a computer all day. Although there are complete online curriculums available for the primary grades, most of them are designed to be used by home-schoolers or on a part-time basis. Most primary classes use online curriculum as a supplement, rather than to replace the entire curriculum.
3. Higher-level courses, such as advanced placement courses, are not suited for the online environment because they do not allow for intense student-to-student interactions and speaking requirements. There is some validity to this argument, so a program may choose to offer some online courses only in a blended format. However, in some cases, an online class may be the only way a student can access the curriculum. For chronically ill students who cannot attend a traditional school or for students in rural areas who lack access to highly qualified teachers in all areas, an online class may be the only option for accessing advanced curriculum. In these cases, sacrificing interaction may be worth providing students with access to content suited to their ability level.

SELECT THE TECHNOLOGY/VENDORS

Now that there is a clear picture of what the program will look like and how it will operate, and key staff have been selected, it is finally time to identify the specific technologies and/or vendors that will be used to launch the program. It is important for the staff to be hired before this step so they have a voice in product selection. A method of evaluation, such as a rubric or checklist, should be developed to rate the products in each category before a request for proposals (RFP) is issued. The rubric should maintain alignment to the vision, mission, and desired attributes for the program.

Vendors should be available to make presentations, conduct demonstrations, and provide full access to their products for trial purposes. Be wary of vendors who will only allow supervised perusal of their products or provide demo accounts that do not allow full access to systems. Staff members should rate each product separately using the rubric and then discuss their ratings as a group before making the final selection. Make sure that all proposals contain careful cost accounting that outlines initial and ongoing costs, including costs for training and technical support.

SUMMARY

The process suggested in this chapter for initial program development will result in thoughtful planning and a smooth implementation for students, parents, and schools. However, the process does not end there. The following chapters include important discussions about program standards and standards monitoring, the design of curriculum, and methods to ensure academic integrity.

NOTES

1. Michael B. Horn, "Is K–12 Blended Learning Disruptive? It Depends," Clayton Christensen Institute for Disruptive Innovation (blog), May 2013, http://www.christenseninstitute.org/is-k-12-blended-learning-disruptive-it-depends/.

2. William and Flora Hewlett Foundation, "Open Educational Resources," accessed November 11, 2013, http://www.hewlett.org/programs/education-program/open-educational-resources.

CHAPTER 3

Curriculum

Purchasing or developing curriculum is one of the most expensive components of a K–12 online program, so it is important to make a wise investment. The development of curriculum for the online setting requires collaboration between curriculum experts, course developers, and programmers, and is an intensely time-consuming task. Because of the cost and time commitment, many schools and programs choose to purchase curriculum from an outside vendor rather than developing curriculum in-house. There are pros and cons to either approach.

OPTIONS FOR CURRICULUM

There are many benefits to the internal development of curriculum, including the potential for long-term cost savings and the freedom to modify curriculum as needed. Although there is a considerable upfront cost to content development, annual subscription or licensing fees are avoided. Programs that choose to develop curriculum can create content that is strictly aligned to state standards and district curriculum maps. The program or district owns the rights to the content, and modifications can be made as needed.

There are also disadvantages to internal curriculum development. Districts or schools that want to move quickly to launch an online program may be unable to wait for curriculum to be developed in-house. In-house curriculum development requires the dedication of personnel resources and significant technical expertise. In addition to content area experts, an online program will need personnel with web authoring, digital video, and programming proficiency.

Internally developed curriculum must be closely monitored for copyright infringement. Classroom teachers are accustomed to liberal copyright allowances for content used for classroom purposes. However, these same allowances do not transfer when curriculum will be placed online. For example, teachers often reproduce articles from newspapers or magazines in print format for classroom use, but copying such an article for an online course would likely be a violation of copyright law.

Purchasing curriculum from a vendor offers the potential to get an online school or program off the ground quickly, but there are several downsides to this approach. Most curriculum vendors develop curriculum for a nationwide audience, and although these vendors will claim specific alignment to state and local standards, alignment is generally done after the fact. Rather than being built upon specific standards, alignment is done by drawing connections between the completed curriculum and state and local standards. Purchasing curriculum from a vendor usually requires the use of a proprietary learning management system (LMS), limiting the flexibility of the product. Subscription or license fees can be costly, and vendors generally charge for additional services like training or technical support. Many online schools and programs start by using third-party curriculum, with the intent of developing their own curriculum in-house simultaneously. Unfortunately, limited resources (money and personnel) within school districts often mean that in-house curriculum is never developed, leaving online programs permanently dependent upon third-party curriculum.

A third option for curriculum is the formation of partnerships between a public school district that has developed its own curriculum and other school districts that want to launch an online program but lack the resources to develop curriculum internally. The Mesa Distance Learning Program (MDLP) in Mesa, Arizona, is an example of this type of partnership. MDLP is a program of the Mesa Unified School District, the largest public school district in Arizona. MDLP develops its entire curriculum internally, based on Arizona state standards and district curriculum maps, and uses a proprietary LMS. MDLP enters into partnerships with other school districts, allowing them to use some or all of the course offerings at a reasonable cost that is much lower than that offered by commercial curriculum vendors. The low-cost yet high-quality curriculum provided by MDLP allows other districts to provide online courses on either a permanent basis or a short-term basis while curriculum is developed internally.

Whether purchasing or developing curriculum, online administrators should consider several important factors:

1. Curriculum should be based upon state and local standards.
2. Curriculum should be appropriate for the grade level.
3. Curriculum should include chunked content and frequent feedback.
4. Curriculum should be flexible and accessible on a variety of devices.
5. Curriculum should include the ability to differentiate instruction for diverse learners.

STANDARDS-BASED CURRICULUM

In the era of high-stakes testing, it is more important than ever for classroom instruction to be aligned to state and local standards—whether the classroom is in a brick-and-mortar school or online. Standards-based instruction is important because students may be required to pass an end-of-course assessment to earn credit or an exit exam to earn a high school diploma. Standards-based instruction is important for teachers and administrators because new evaluation frameworks often require districts to include quantitative data on student academic progress that accounts for a significant portion of each evaluation outcome. With so much resting upon student achievement for students, teachers, and administrators, online program administrators should be careful to choose curriculum that addresses the learning goals mandated by their district.

As mentioned earlier in this chapter, commercial curriculum vendors create generic curriculum intended to appeal to a wide audience, and then demonstrate alignment to specific state and local standards after the fact. In some cases, vendors can show strong alignment between curriculum and standards—especially in the lessons they have selected for demonstration purposes. However, before making the decision to purchase curriculum, program administrators would be wise to demand full access to all courses for a preview period, giving local content area experts time to peruse the curriculum and determine whether all standards are adequately addressed. Some vendors make the claim that content can be modified if all local standards are not addressed. However, curriculum modification often carries a hefty price tag.

Programs that choose to develop curriculum internally have the luxury of ensuring that all content is built from the ground up based on state standards and local curriculum maps. Backward design is the best approach for developing content. This method of designing educational curriculum involves setting learning goals before choosing instructional methods and forms of assessment.[1] Backward design of curriculum typically involves three stages:

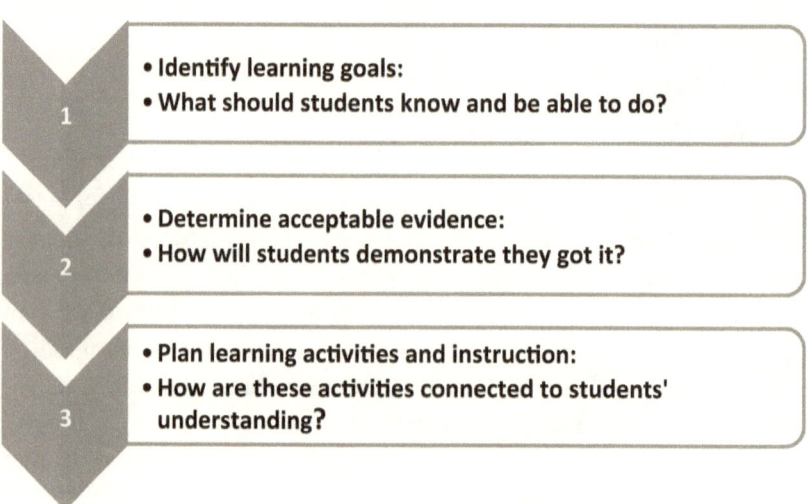

Figure 3.1.

Using the backward design method helps ensure that all learning activities are meaningful, worthwhile, and aligned to the standards.

GRADE-LEVEL APPROPRIATE

Good classroom teachers are adept at creating lessons that will appeal to the age level of their audience. However, online classroom teachers are often not involved in the development of curriculum and are at the mercy of curriculum developers to ensure that lessons are grade-level appropriate. Several factors make curriculum grade-level appropriate: readability, learning strategies, cross-curricular connections, and types of examples used to illustrate concepts. Commercial curriculum vendors usually offer content-based courses intended for school groups, such as middle school American history or high school world history. However, there can be a great difference in maturity between a high school freshman and a high school senior. When previewing curriculum, the selection committee should carefully consider the grade-level appropriateness of any course.

CHUNKED CURRICULUM AND FREQUENT FEEDBACK

An essential strategy in the design of an effective online course is content chunking, or the breaking of course content into smaller pieces to allow learners to process, practice, and retain the information. How the content will be chunked is determined by several factors, including the subject area (language arts, math, science, social studies, etc.), the grade level, and the target audience (regular, credit recovery, honors). Course developers with subject area expertise and classroom teaching experience should be able to appropriately chunk the content. Content chunking involves dividing the actual content into smaller pieces and then providing some means of practice and a check for understanding. Students should receive feedback during each chunk of content that identifies the need for remediation or signals that the student is ready to move on to the next chunk.

In an online course, chunked content is important because it breaks subject matter down into manageable pieces and increases student engagement. Teachers in a classroom frequently check in with students to assess understanding by asking questions, listening to discussions, or observing student behavior. Content chunks in an online course should include some method of student engagement that demands student interaction with the content. Online lessons that lack frequent opportunities for students to interact with the content cannot ensure student engagement and do not allow for the formative assessment of key concepts.

The importance of feedback in the learning process cannot be understated; it is the means by which students know where they are in the learning process. Feedback identifies what students are doing right and what they need to work on next, which means that it should be frequent and ongoing. An effective online course will provide multiple ways for students to receive both automated and teacher-generated feedback on a regular basis.

Automated, or computer-generated, feedback is best used for lower-level thinking tasks. If a student does not demonstrate mastery on a learning check, some method of remediation should be applied. If students are receiving automated feedback on smaller chunks of learning throughout a unit or lesson and are given the opportunity for remediation, it increases the likelihood that the student will be successful on the major learning goal. Results from automated feedback should be provided to the teacher of the course in addition to the student to allow the teacher to detect patterns and offer additional remediation as needed.

Effective online course design also includes learning activities that require higher-level thinking skills and demand teacher-generated feedback. Like automated feedback, teacher-generated feedback should be frequent and ongoing. For example, the first time a student receives teacher-generated feedback on a writing assignment should not be when the final essay is submitted. Rather, the student should be conferring with the teacher throughout the writing process to ensure the best possible outcome on the final essay.

Feedback, whether automated or teacher-generated, should encourage students to reflect on their own learning. The learning goal for each unit and lesson should be clear, and students should understand how to connect their results on each learning check to the overall goal. The inclusion of grading checklists and rubrics is an effective way to guide students into self-reflection. Students can use the checklist or rubric to assess their own work and compare their score to the teacher's score. Teachers must help students learn the process of self-reflection and require that it be done throughout the course.

When choosing curriculum, program administrators should look for course design that provides ongoing, frequent feedback that is both automated and teacher-generated, and demands continual self-reflection.

FLEXIBILITY AND ACCESSIBILITY

Ever-changing content standards mean that it is imperative for online schools and programs to have the ability to modify content. When choosing a curriculum provider, it is important to determine whether content can be modified. Consider these important questions regarding curriculum modification:

- Who is responsible for the modification—the school or the curriculum provider?
- What costs are associated with content modification?
- What happens if it is determined that a particular lesson, unit, or course is not effective?

Technology changes even more quickly than content standards. In this context, accessibility refers to the ability to access content on a variety of devices using a variety of operating systems: laptop computers, desktop computers, tablets, smartphones, and other mobile devices. Many curriculum providers have developed online content that is reliant on browser plug-ins like Flash or QuickTime that will not work on tablets and other mobile devices. It is wise to select a curriculum provider who is designing for the most current technology standards and will allow students to access online courses on a variety of devices.

DIFFERENTIATING INSTRUCTION FOR DIVERSE LEARNERS

Effective teachers differentiate instruction to meet the needs of diverse learners. In a classroom, it may be possible to differentiate instruction on demand as the need arises, but in the online setting, differentiation requires thoughtful planning to be incorporated into curriculum design. The term *universal design for learning* (UDL) is defined by the Higher Education Opportunity Act as:

> "a scientifically valid framework for guiding educational practice that—
> (A) provides flexibility in the ways information is presented, in the ways students respond or demonstrate knowledge and skills, and in the ways students are engaged; and (B) reduces barriers in instruction,

provides appropriate accommodations, supports, and challenges, and maintains high achievement expectations for all students, including students with disabilities and students who are limited English proficient."[2]

The goal of UDL is to create curriculum that meets the needs of all learners with flexible designs and customizable options. The underlying principles of UDL should be considered when designing or selecting online curriculum:

1. The curriculum should provide multiple means of representation, or the "what" of learning. Online curriculum should include options for the transfer of information to compensate for the different ways that learners perceive and comprehend information. For example, how will a blind student or a student with poor reading comprehension skills access online text? In these cases, students will need access to a text-to-speech reader or other audio component, which should be built into the course design. Other learners may be able to access online text without audio but would benefit from a graphic illustration of key concepts. One means of representation will not work for all learners, making it essential to provide multiple means of representation.
2. The curriculum should provide multiple means of action and expression, or the "how" of learning. Physical limitations, learning disabilities, or differences in learning styles mean that learners differ in the ways they can express what they know. Effective curriculum design should provide options for action and expression.
3. The curriculum should provide multiple means of engagement, or the "why" of learning. Motivating students to learn and helping them remain engaged in learning is difficult in the online environment, particularly when students are working from a remote location and are not under the direct supervision of a teacher. The online course structure should provide flexibility to address different styles of engagement, such as options for collaboration with peers or independent work. The ability for students to work at their own pace and direct their own learning should be balanced with the appropriate structure, such as course pacing guidelines and calendars.[3]

Differentiating instruction requires thoughtful planning and increases course development time. However, building differentiation into the course design at the outset will save time and money in the long run by preventing the need for revisions after the fact. Some programs choose to provide differentiation options to all students, while others choose to make options available to students on an as-needed basis. It is important to note that for students with individualized education plans (IEPs) and 504 plans, differentiation is not a choice. Schools and programs that fail to provide options for these students may face legal action. Overall, differentiating instruction is an effective teaching strategy for all students.

SUMMARY

Choosing curriculum for an online program is a critical decision because it impacts student learning and achievement, and requires a significant investment in terms of money and personnel. The first step in making this choice is determining whether curriculum will be developed internally or purchased from a vendor. Whether purchasing curriculum or developing curriculum, the final product should be standards-based and grade-level appropriate, demand student engagement, provide consistent feedback, be accessible on a variety of devices, and differentiate instruction for diverse learners.

NOTES

1. Jay McTighe and Grant Wiggins, *Understanding by Design: Professional Development Workbook* (Alexandria: Association for Supervision and Curriculum Development, 2004), 12.

2. Higher Education Opportunity Act, Pub. L. No. 107-296 (2008), http://www.gpo.gov/fdsys/pkg/PLAW-110publ315/pdf/PLAW-110publ315.pdf.

3. National Center on Universal Design for Learning, "What Is UDL?," last modified April 17, 2013, http://www.udlcenter.org/aboutudl/whatisudl.

CHAPTER 4

The Potential Impact of the Common Core

Forcing a square peg into a round hole is an apt description of the attempt to make accountability systems designed for brick-and-mortar schools work in an online setting. The idea of accountability—holding not only students but teachers, schools, even school districts accountable for student performance—has been prevalent in public education for several decades, and the latest iteration is tied to the Common Core State Standards Initiative (CCSSI). Accountability in schools is a controversial topic and creates challenges for any school. Online schools and programs, however, face unique challenges when attempting to adhere to the inflexible procedures mandated by school accountability systems. The goal of accountability is increased student achievement, but applying the current system to online schools may eliminate a primary advantage of online learning—flexibility.

The accountability movement has lofty goals: quantifying the effectiveness of schools and identifying where resources are not equitably distributed. Standards are established to determine what students should know and be able to do, and tests are developed to measure whether the goals identified by the standard were achieved. The accountability concept, in theory, is sound, but implementing a system that actually leads to increased student achievement has been problematic. Over the past three decades, multiple sets of standards and assessments have been created.

THE CORE OF THE COMMON CORE

The current CCSSI was launched by the National Governors Association (NGA) and Council of Chief State School Officers (CCSSO) in 2008. Members of these organizations were concerned that high school graduates lacked basic skills that prepared them for higher education or the world of work, and decided to push for a common, rigorous curriculum in all the states to ensure students could succeed in college and their careers. It is important to note that the Common Core standards have been adopted by forty-five states, making the CCSSI more of a national reform effort.

The CCSSI elevates the rigor of the standards in math and English language arts and holds teachers responsible for teaching higher-level thinking skills. Although the standards are specific to math and English language arts, the NGA and CCSSO envisioned more reading, discussion, writing, and speaking in all K–12 classrooms. The CCSSI changes the curriculum for math and English language arts but also requires a pedagogical change in all curricular areas—a lofty goal, indeed.

HIGH-STAKES TESTS

A high-stakes test used for accountability is a critical element of the CCSSI. Assessments are being developed by many organizations and vendors, including the Partnership for Assessment of Readiness for College and Careers (PARCC) and the Smarter Balanced Assessment Consortium (SBAC). CCSSI member states are hopeful that these assessments are accurate measures of achievement of the Common Core standards, because past efforts to develop high-stakes tests have been expensive and plagued with problems. The intent is for PARCC- and SBAC-designed tests to be administered online; the costs for technology to support the testing process will be epic. Whether schools will be able to raise the funds for the initial expense and sustain the ongoing maintenance costs is questionable.

An overhaul of teacher and administrator evaluation systems occurred simultaneously with the CCSSI movement. The Race to the Top (RTT) federal grant competition was announced in 2009, with a major goal of "recruiting, evaluating, and retaining highly effective teachers and principals."[1] RTT called for states to develop new teacher evaluation systems that included specific components: evaluating teacher effectiveness using multiple rating categories and taking into account data on student growth. These new evaluation systems were often tied to revised pay-for-performance structures based on the achievement of students. In these structures, data on student growth comes from a high-stakes test, and the frequency of teacher observations is increased.

THE COMMON CORE DRIVES CHANGES

The implementation of the CCSSI and the associated high-stakes testing is forcing educators to rethink the approach to teaching. Although the stated purpose of the standards is to "provide a consistent, clear understanding of what students are expected to learn, so teachers and parents know what they need to do to help them," school districts and local schools are scrambling to define what should be taught and how it should be delivered to ensure that students are prepared for the high-stakes assessments aligned to the CCSSI.[2] Educators are accustomed to ever-changing standards; a change in state content-based standards often means altering the timeline for teaching a particular unit or lesson. However, implementation of the CCSSI mandates a complete redesign of unit and lesson plans.

The CCSSI should have a significant impact on online programs—if programs implement the standards with fidelity. Synchronous and district-level programs will face fewer obstacles to implementation than asynchronous and national programs, but all programs will be challenged to implement the Common Core as intended.

ALIGNMENT OF COMMON CORE STANDARDS IN ONLINE PROGRAMS

The issue of alignment to the Common Core standards deserves careful scrutiny in the online classroom. Nationwide online curriculum providers are accustomed to "adapting" their products to various state standards by showing connections to specific state content-based standards in established curriculum. For any curriculum to be truly aligned to a set of standards, the curriculum should be built from the ground up, with the standards serving as the foundation. It is easy to make a theoretical alignment using words, but it is much more difficult to truly align the instructional process with specific standards.

The CCSSI means that online curriculum providers must develop new curriculum in the areas of math and English language arts and make substantial modifications to other content areas. In the frenzy to claim alignment to the Common Core, for-profit curriculum providers are more likely to make minor modifications to existing products, rather than develop new curriculum that substantially increases rigor and provides for more interaction. For-profit online programs employ powerful lobbyists, and it is likely these connections will be used in state legislatures to minimize the impact of the Common Core on for-profit programs.

Schools and programs interested in purchasing online curriculum must demonstrate due diligence in vetting the curriculum. Be leery of vendors who are only willing to show a chart that demonstrates alignment between lessons and standards, or restrict previewing access to units and lessons of the vendor's choosing. True alignment to the Common Core standards is more than an alignment of words; the curriculum should reflect an emphasis on critical reading, writing, and thinking and an elevated level of interaction.

IMPLICATIONS FOR LESSON DESIGN IN ONLINE PROGRAMS

The CCSSI places high cognitive demands on students by expecting them to comprehend texts of increased complexity; make reasoned judgments; construct viable, evidence-based arguments; communicate effectively through speech and writing; and persevere in their learning. To accommodate these demands, course developers must find ways to compensate for the lack of face-to-face interaction for students.

Prior to the CCSSI, most asynchronous online programs used a simple format for lesson design. After the curriculum was established, lessons and courses were developed based on objectives/standards. The content was usually presented in a linear text format, perhaps with short videos in some areas. Student understanding was assessed formatively through assignments and tests, and a summative final examination was administered at the end of the course. In most cases, student engagement and collaboration were minimal, and a minimal amount of writing was completed in non-English language arts courses.

This format was efficient and provided an easy way for students to complete a course. Students rushed to sign up for these courses as they were fairly easy and could be completed quickly. In some programs, a course could be completed in a few weeks. Most public school (nonprofit) programs developed courses for the same amount of instructional time required in a brick-and-mortar school.

Lesson design for Common Core alignment in the asynchronous environment should emphasize three components:

1. Rich teacher-student dialogue based on specific, meaningful, and timely teacher feedback.
2. Strategies to scaffold and differentiate learning.
3. Opportunities for students to revise and modify until key concepts have been mastered.

The ongoing conversation between the online teacher and student is especially important when students do not have the benefit of regular classroom discussion. Teachers should use the conversation to help students identify misconceptions or holes in their learning, prompt higher-level thinking or extend learning, offer encouragement, and help students formulate questions. Feedback should not only serve as an explanation for a grade on an assessment, but also be used throughout the course as a learning tool. Effective feedback is connected to iterative learning; students may need multiple opportunities to master important skills or concepts.

OPTIONS FOR K–12 ONLINE PROGRAMS

It is likely that implementation of the Common Core will force most online schools and programs to change their model of operating. To accommodate the demands of the Common Core, programs may consider using one or more options: a cohort-based enrollment system, a synchronous approach, or a blended approach.

1. A significant change would be from an open-entry to a cohort-based enrollment system, driven by PARCC and/or SBAC assessments. These tests are designed to be end-of-course assessments, administered during the last weeks of the school year. An advantage of online learning is flexibility; many programs operate asynchronously so they can offer open enrollment. It would be unfair to force a student who recently started a course to take a high-stakes end-of-course assessment. A potential result may be that online programs are forced to enroll students according to a traditional school schedule, reducing options for students with special circumstances.
2. A synchronous environment allows for some collaboration through the use of group assignments, threaded discussions, and real-time web conferencing. Students are expected to follow the same pacing calendar, making it possible to require some type of collaboration. A synchronous design would be used in tandem with a cohort-based enrollment system, greatly reducing the flexibility for students with special circumstances. Online learning is often chosen at the K–12 level because of its flexibility; the open-entry nature of an asynchronous environment allows it to be used to suit individual learning and for students with special circumstances.
3. Online courses previously used for independent learning could be used in a blended setting to provide for more student-to-student interaction. This integration may well become the most popular use of online programs in the future. Students may spend some time working independently online, either in a classroom or at home, reading texts, watching videos, participating in interactive modules, or completing assessments. Teachers would monitor student progress online and determine when individual or small-group activities, such as discussion, tutoring, or presentations, were needed. Lab space is required for this approach, but it allows for the reallocation of existing online resources. Some schools currently offer students the opportunity to take an online class during a period of the regular school day by reporting to

a computer lab staffed by a certified teacher or lab assistant. In this setting, students take classes from different curriculum areas, depending upon their specific needs. The lab assistant or teacher can provide support in terms of using the technology or study skills, but may not be able to provide content-specific support. This approach may be modified to support the Common Core by grouping students by core area, such as math or English language arts, and staffing the lab with a highly qualified teacher. The teacher could structure small- or whole-group activities to build in interaction and allow students to practice speaking skills.

A final option some online schools and programs may choose is to make nominal changes to existing structures and curriculum and hope that resistance to the Common Core results in its repeal.

THE BOTTOM LINE—INCREASED COST

Online learning is an attractive option to many school districts because it can be less expensive, but the transition to the CCSSI has the potential to significantly increase the cost of course delivery. An emphasis on teacher-student interaction and a mastery- or competency-based learning approach will increase the amount of time invested by the online teacher per student. Although pay structures vary for online teaching, it is likely that teachers must either be paid for an increase in time or provide services to a smaller number of students.

The cost increase for teacher salaries can be mitigated with thoughtful course design by allowing for automated feedback for lower-level thinking and content-acquisition tasks. However, the cost to deliver an online course will increase, whether a district pays its own teachers to teach online courses or pays a course fee to another provider that includes the teacher's cost.

Successful implementation of the CCSSI also requires ongoing professional development for teachers. Districts across the nation recognize the need for targeted professional development for teachers in brick-and-mortar schools, and the same approach is needed for online schools and programs. Initial training should be provided to new teachers and existing staff when curriculum updates are made, and sustained throughout the teacher's tenure in the online classroom. On-demand professional development supplied through videos and/or a text-based format is essential for teachers who work remotely.

Other costs will also increase. Transitioning from a fully online to a blended model or increasing student support in a blended model will require personnel and physical resources. Modification of curriculum requires the services of teachers, curriculum developers, and programmers. These increased costs are likely to be passed on from external providers to the schools that buy the services.

IS THE COMMON CORE HERE TO STAY?

Like previous school reform and accountability movements, the CCSSI has critics. Some conservatives believe that the Common Core standards replace local control with a federally mandated curriculum, and pressure from this conservative element is already causing some politicians to back away from the standards. One example of the conservative backlash is a resolution released by the Republican National Committee in April 2013, calling the Common Core an "inappropriate overreach to standardize and control the education of our children."[3] Criticism also has also been levied about the high cost of implementation; full implementation requires professional development, updated resources, new technology, and a new and expensive high-stakes test.

Community resistance from parents and other stakeholders develops when they feel excluded from the standards adoption process and do not understand how the changes will impact their children. A 2013 Phi Delta Kappa/Gallup Poll indicated a widespread lack of knowledge regarding the Common Core: "Slightly more than one-third of Americans have ever heard of the Common Core; among Americans with children in public schools, fewer than half recognized the Core."[4] The same poll also revealed that among the people who had heard of the Common Core, a majority did not believe that the standards would improve the quality of education in America.

Supporters of the Common Core maintain that opponents of the standards are misinformed, and most schools are following through with implementation despite the controversy. Some schools are trying to defuse the controversy by communicating with parents and students regarding the increased level of rigor. Despite these efforts, parents are likely to be concerned when their children are unable to achieve at the same level while doing what they have always done.

Real-life examples of parent complaints illustrate the potential for strong community resistance to the Common Core. A mother of an elementary school–aged child in Mesa, Arizona, called the school to complain about the new way of teaching. Her son, previously an above-average student, came home with his first report card of the school year with two Ds and three Fs. A parent of a high school–aged student enrolled in an online program lodged a complaint regarding a teacher's persistence in questioning techniques that demanded critical thinking. This parent demanded a return to curriculum that allowed the student to earn high marks for tasks that emphasized content acquisition and required minimal interaction with the teacher. Parent resistance will solidify as children struggle with the cognitive demands of the Common Core.

The real test for the permanence of the CCSSI will occur when the first set of PARCC and SBAC results is released, as it is widely anticipated that these scores will demonstrate a dramatic drop in student achievement from previous tests. Previous attempts to use high-stakes tests for accountability purposes have resulted in finger-pointing and a lowering of the standards. People begin to question the system to determine the reason for the low scores, and no group wants to accept responsibility. In some cases, minimum passing rates are lowered in response to public pressure, undermining the effort to improve student achievement. It remains to be seen if states will withstand the challenges and give the CCSSI time to prove that it can elevate the level of rigor and student achievement across the nation.

SUMMARY

Online programs and schools that plan to align teaching and learning to the Common Core should prepare for curriculum modification, an increase in cost, and a change in the delivery model. The only option is to wait and see if Common Core goes the way of previous school reform and accountability attempts and gradually fades away, only to be replaced with the next accountability concept.

NOTES

1. U.S. Department of Education, "Race to the Top Executive Summary," November 2009, http://www2.ed.gov/programs/racetothetop/executive-summary.pdf.

2. Common Core State Standards Initiative, accessed September 15, 2012, http://www.corestandards.org/.

3. Republican National Committee, "Resolution Concerning Common Core Education Standards," April 12, 2013, http://www.gop.com/wp-content/uploads/2013/07/Resolution_Concerning_Common_Core_Education_Standards.pdf.

4. William J. Bushaw and Shane J. Lopez, "The 45th Annual PDK/Gallup Poll of the Public's Attitudes Toward the Public Schools," Phi Delta Kappa International, August 21, 2013, http://pdkintl.org/noindex/2013_PDKGallup.pdf.

CHAPTER 5

Academic Integrity

Cheating within online programs is the elephant in the room; everybody knows it is a problem, but the issue is rarely discussed. A recent conference for the International Council for Online Learning (iNACOL)—the largest conference dedicated to online education—included close to 400 breakout sessions, but not one addressed the topic of academic integrity. Most online programs and vendors claim a system is used to detect academic misconduct, but the practices range from very weak, loose systems to detailed, strong detection systems where final examinations are proctored and students must pass the final examination to receive course credit.

WHAT IS ACADEMIC INTEGRITY?

Academic integrity is an assurance that grades are honestly earned by the student. Academic integrity exists when students seek knowledge honestly and fairly. Academic dishonesty occurs when students plagiarize, submit work done by others as their own, or use unauthorized resources on an exam or other assessment. It is essential for programs to have procedures in place to ensure high standards of academic integrity, because academic dishonesty impedes learning that leads to success at the next level. Other educational institutions accept earned credits and respect the character of an online program when there are appropriate systems in place to ensure academic integrity.

ACADEMIC INTEGRITY BUILDS CREDIBILITY

The accountability and credibility of online programs are dependent upon a strong system to maintain academic integrity. A system of academic integrity defines the character of an online program and helps it build a strong reputation. The failure of some programs to have such systems in place tarnishes the reputation of all programs, and could be the single practice that diminishes the standing of online education within communities and among institutions of higher learning. As explained in a recent policy brief from the National Education Policy Center at the University of Colorado, Boulder: "The lack of face-to-face relationships between students and teachers can lead to abuses that threaten the legitimacy of the entire institution of cyber-schooling."[1] How individual programs address this issue will determine the collective future of online education at the K–12 level. Without some assurance that the person doing the work is the same person who earns the credit, online programs lack credibility and accountability, especially with other educational institutions and the military.

The Mesa Distance Learning Program (MDLP) took a strong stance regarding academic integrity from its inception, and has developed a reputation throughout the state of Arizona as a rigorous and credible program. Over the years, some students who have graduated from other online charter schools in the state have contacted MDLP about the possibility of "redoing" high school through MDLP because a military recruiter refused the diploma from the online charter school. Insufficient systems for ensuring academic integrity in some online programs resulted in changes in the way online courses are evaluated by the National Collegiate Athletic Association (NCAA). It even appears that students and parents are aware that a diploma from some online programs is inferior. It is common for students who attend online charter schools to attempt to transfer back to a public school shortly before graduation, because they know that a public school diploma carries greater credibility.

The road taken as a distance learning community—including charter, district, and private programs—will either garner greater respect for online education or serve as further evidence that online programs are less effective at preparing students for the next level of learning or the world of work. Strong academic integrity practices will ensure growth for virtual programs. Programs with a reputation of being "credit mills" where little work or time is required to receive a transcript will increase the base of disbelievers who question the role of online courses in K–12 education.

How can it be assured that the student enrolled in a course(s) is the same person who is doing the work, taking the final examination, and earning the credit? The answer to this question determines the strength of the academic integrity system in an online program.

SHIFTING SOCIETAL VIEW OF CHEATING

Many educators would agree that a values shift regarding cheating has occurred in society; cheating is no longer considered unethical or immoral. For some students and parents, the end justifies the means—as long as the desired grade is achieved, then it does not matter how the result was accomplished. Online teachers have even reported cases in which parents were complicit with academic dishonesty. Some online programs avoid taking a firm position on academic integrity to avoid confrontations with students and parents.

A counselor in a small town in Arizona exemplified this attitude when he declined to address an issue of academic misconduct in an online course. According to the counselor, the parents and the school administration just wanted the student to graduate, whether the credit was earned honestly or otherwise. Despite the lack of support from some parents, advocates at the National Education Policy Center recommend a firm stance against academic dishonesty: "Students in virtual learning environments need to be held to the same standards prohibiting cheating and plagiarism as students in traditional classroom environment."[2] Educators have an obligation to maintain high standards for all students and model appropriate behavior, even when faced with challenging situations.

THE POLITICS OF CHEATING

In Arizona, a group of stakeholders (charter and district school programs) attended a legislative meeting where the issue of academic integrity in online education was discussed. The district schools advocated mandatory proctored final exams for online programs, and some even recommended that passing the final exam should be a requirement to earn credit for the course. A lobbyist representing a well-known national charter school suggested an alternative: online courses should include multiple assessments throughout the course and all mandatory state testing would be proctored.

The lobbyist's suggestion was akin to requiring that all cars and trucks on the freeway must have wheels. All reputable courses include multiple assessments, and the only mandatory test in Arizona was the test required for high school graduation that is always proctored under strict conditions. Nonetheless, the wording was added to the state statutes for online education, even though it had no impact on how online schools functioned and failed to increase standards of academic integrity.

Most online programs have academic integrity policy statements. Unfortunately, like the state statute in Arizona, for some programs these statements exist only to provide an illusion of academic integrity. It is up to students, parents, and school personnel to conduct due diligence when selecting online providers to ensure they are choosing a program that maintains high standards in all areas, including academic integrity.

In Arizona, the issue of academic integrity reached a boiling point when credits from substandard charter schools were refused by other K–12 educational entities, institutions of higher learning, and the military. Instead of improving their practices, the charter schools sought help from the state legislature. The charter school lobbyists were successful in securing passage of a law that forced Arizona schools to accept credits from any accredited school—charter or district.

District schools refused credits from substandard online programs for good reason; the credits were not representative of true learning, and the courses did not prepare students for success at the next level. For example, consider a student who earned an Algebra I credit through a substandard online institution but had not mastered basic concepts necessary for success in Algebra II in a district school classroom. To deal with this problem, some districts required students to pass the district end-of-course assessment in order to transfer in the credit from an online program. If the student was unable to pass the district end-of-course assessment, the credit would be accepted in accordance with state regulations, but only as an elective credit.

LEADERSHIP FROM THE STATE

In Arizona, oversight of online programs is the responsibility of the state board of education, the superintendent of public instruction, and the state board for charter schools for online charter schools. Leadership from these groups is lacking, and this problem is not limited to Arizona. In 2007, the Arizona Office of the Auditor General's report made the following recommendation regarding academic integrity: "Two practices to help ensure academic integrity are requiring students to take exams in person in a proctored setting and requiring them to pass course exams to receive credit."[3] The audit by the Arizona Office of the Auditor General made many recommendations, and to this day some of those recommendations, such as this one, have never been implemented. The lack of oversight in online education may continue for many years, so it remains the responsibility of individual schools and programs to define the character of their own programs and do the right thing for students.

HOW EASY IS IT TO CHEAT?

The auditor general conducted an audit of the online programs operating in Arizona in 2007—the first and last audit ever conducted on online schools in Arizona. The report stated: "With limited face-to-face contact between students and teachers, ensuring academic integrity is a challenge for online schools."[4] There are four primary methods used by students involved in academic misconduct:

1. Use of unauthorized resources on quizzes and tests.
2. Plagiarism from online sources and other students.
3. Having other people complete course work and assessments.
4. Inappropriate collaboration.

Online programs should employ multiple measures to prevent, monitor, and respond to these and other methods of academic misconduct.

ENSURING ACADEMIC INTEGRITY

The following list contains recommendations for establishing a strong system to ensure academic integrity.

1. Articulate a clear policy that defines academic integrity, provides examples of academic misconduct, and explains the consequences for the failure to adhere to the academic integrity policy.
2. Require completion of an academic integrity module before students can access an online class.
3. Require students to show photo identification to take the final exam.
4. Require students to pass a proctored final exam to earn credit for a course.
5. Make sure all final examinations are proctored by a staff member or by a proctor approved by the program. Ideally, exams should be proctored in a school or other public building. Proctors other than school personnel must be carefully vetted.
6. Active test proctoring should occur in the final exam testing room. If possible, install security cameras in the testing room to discourage misconduct and add another layer of supervision. Recordings should be kept for at least a month.
7. Use external tools, such as Turnitin, to check for plagiarism.
8. Embed internal tools to check for plagiarism on course assignments, such as watermarks on written documents. Watermarks can be used to send an alert to a teacher when a student attempts to submit a document that is the original work of another student.
9. Use testing software that includes security features to show if students access unauthorized resources while taking quizzes and tests.
10. Quiz and test questions should be pulled from a bank of items to ensure that all students do not receive the same questions on an assessment. This also provides flexibility for offering the option of test retakes.

No system is 100 percent effective at preventing academic misconduct. Some students will find ways to deceive and beat the system, but the number of incidents is greatly reduced when procedures such as these are implemented. When MDLP first began operation in 1999, about 30 percent of the students attempted to cheat. After implementing an academic integrity system, only about 5 percent of students engaged in academic misconduct.

Recognition of the fact that no system is foolproof is the reason that MDLP requires students to take a proctored final examination. Student achievement data collected over the years reveals that in most cases, there is a strong correlation between grades on course work and final exams. When there is a discrepancy (90 percent average on course work, 30 percent on final exam), then there is a strong probability that academic misconduct on course work was involved. A requirement for students to pass the proctored final exam to earn course credit is the cornerstone of the MDLP academic integrity policy.

Many programs claim to require proctored final exams, but the difference is the definition of "proctored final examinations." The report by the Arizona Office of the Auditor General revealed: "Four of the state's six largest online schools don't require school-supervised final examinations."[5] At the time of the report, these programs accounted for 83 percent of enrollment in state-approved online schools. It is easy to see how the accountability of online education could be questioned when there is little monitoring for a large majority of the state's online population.

CONSEQUENCES FOR CHEATING

A major component of any academic integrity system is identifying the consequences for academic misconduct. A sample consequence chart is shown below.

The bank of consequences and how they are applied should be consistent with policies and procedures already in place in districts and schools. The MDLP leadership team determined that in some cases, a warning is appropriate for the first offense of academic misconduct. For example, students often do not believe that copying wording directly from course lessons constitutes plagiarism. Teachers can use these situations as learning experiences to help students develop a

Occurrence	1st	2nd	3rd
Logical Consequences	√ Warning explaining rules and consequences sent by teacher via message box √ Written Assignment (worksheets, study guides, essays, etc.): Marked as 'incomplete' and unlocked for student to rewrite/resubmit for grading √ Quiz/Test/Final Exam: Zero issued for any quiz/test/final exam that involves navigating to other lessons – teacher must view activity log to determine which lessons were accessed √ Specialist contacted (if zero issued)	√ Message explaining rules and consequences sent by teacher via message box √ Specialist contacted √ Any written assignment/quiz/test/final exam: Mandatory zero issued, no opportunity for rewrite/resubmission √ Parents contacted by teacher or specialist via phone or email √ Notes placed in hidden comments and/or anecdotal record √ Doug contacted regarding situation	√ Message explaining rules and consequences sent by teacher via message box √ Specialist contacted √ Any written assignment/quiz/test/final exam: Mandatory zero issued, no opportunity for rewrite/resubmission √ Parents contacted by teacher or specialist via phone or email √ Student may be dropped from course √ Notes placed in hidden comments and/or anecdotal record √ Doug contacted regarding situation

* Occurrence = Violation of academic integrity regardless of number of assignments (i.e. If first occurrence involves five written assignments, student is allowed to rewrite/resubmit all five assignments. This is considered one occurrence not five.)

Figure 5.1.
Source: Included with permission of the Mesa Public Schools.

complete understanding of academic integrity and plagiarism. After being reprimanded for the first offense, most students proceed through the course without additional incidents of academic misconduct. Occasionally, students continue to engage in academic misconduct and an escalation of consequences is required, sometimes even resulting in a loss of credit for the course.

Once a process for dealing with academic misconduct has been established, it is critical that the procedures be applied consistently to all students. In years past, parents would work with the MDLP staff to change student behavior. Today, it is not uncommon for parents to support their students and challenge the consequences even though the evidence of misconduct is very clear. Making an exception to established procedures to placate a noisy parent is a slippery slope that leads to more exceptions and the weakening of the entire academic integrity system. When reasonable consequences are applied based on clear evidence, it is easy to stand firm when faced with a challenge.

REMOVING THE INCENTIVE TO CHEAT

Given that cheating is easier in the online setting than in the traditional classroom, and that the societal view of cheating seems to be shifting to one of acceptance, it makes sense that rather than focusing entirely on preventing, monitoring, and punishing academic misconduct, online programs should focus on removing the incentive to cheat. Why do students cheat? For some students, cheating is the easiest or only way to achieve a desired goal, such as earning a credit or raising a grade, and to avoid the punitive consequences that result from failure. Students cheat when the emphasis is placed on grades rather than learning, or when they doubt their own ability to be successful at a task.

In addition to developing a strong system for academic integrity, online programs can deter academic misconduct by making learning the focus in all courses. Traditional quiz and test formats, such as multiple choice and fill in the blank, should be used to provide immediate feedback to students regarding their progress toward a learning goal, but not as the primary source of information to determine an overall grade in the course. Instead, ask students to complete authentic assessments in a risk-free environment by providing them the opportunity to revise and resubmit work until the learning goal is achieved. Authentic assessments can generally be broken down into steps, allowing for specific teacher feedback along the way, making it more difficult to copy from another student and more likely that the student can be successful on the final product.

SUMMARY

This chapter raised important questions related to the credibility and accountability of online schools and programs:

1. Why is the whole idea of ensuring that the enrolled student is doing the work and earning credit not discussed in professional circles?
2. Why do some programs ignore academic misconduct?
3. Why do accreditation agencies give the stamp of approval to programs that do not ensure academic integrity?
4. Where is the monitoring of existing programs from state education departments?
5. What can schools and programs do to prevent and monitor academic misconduct?

As it stands, it is up to individual schools and programs to monitor themselves to ensure student learning. Programs must develop a comprehensive academic integrity system to ensure that students who earn credits in an online class are prepared for the next step in life.

NOTES

1. Gene V. Glass and Kevin G. Welner, *Online K–12 Schooling in the U.S.: Uncertain Private Ventures in Need of Public Regulation* (Boulder, CO: National Education Policy Center, October 2011), accessed April 1, 2014, http://nepc.colorado.edu/publication/online-k-12-schooling.
2. Justin Bathon, *Model Legislation Related to Online Learning Opportunities for Students in Public Elementary and Secondary Education Schools*

(Boulder, CO: National Education Policy Center, 2011), accessed April 1, 2014, http://nepc.colorado.edu/publication/online-K-12-schooling.

3. State of Arizona Office of the Auditor General, *Technology Assisted Project-Based Instruction Program* 37.

4. Ibid., 32.

5. Ibid., 32.

CHAPTER 6

Evaluating Online Teachers and Specialists

The evaluation of classroom teachers is dependent upon a cycle of observation and conferencing; at first thought, it seems like it would be simple to transfer this process to the online classroom. A dynamic user interface and learning management system will allow administrators to review different elements of the teaching process, such as student-teacher dialogue, activity logs, and samples of student work. However, variances in online teaching make it difficult to develop observation protocols that will work for all situations: blended or fully online, synchronous or asynchronous, open-entry or cohort-based. The complexities of observing online teachers cannot be used as an excuse to avoid evaluation altogether, because teacher evaluation is critical for accountability and professional growth. An effective evaluation framework for online teaching should be structured according to four principles:

1. The evaluation tool should be aligned to program expectations and the school/district evaluation framework.
2. The evaluation instrument should include both qualitative and quantitative measures.
3. The evaluation process should provide accountability and lead to professional growth.
4. The evaluation process should not penalize online teachers for variances from classroom teaching.

Many school districts attempt to evaluate online and traditional teachers using the same instrument. Traditional teacher evaluation instruments were never a good fit for the online classroom, but the problem intensified after the Race to the Top (RTT) initiative was announced in 2009. After the passage of RTT, states embarked on school reform initiatives that aligned with RTT principles, including new mandates for teacher and principal evaluations. School districts had flexibility in creating their own evaluation instruments, but the end product had to include both a standards-based and a value-added component. Standards-based evaluations focus on data-driven class observations and relate to an explicit and well-defined rubric based on district standards.[1] The value-added approach is quantitative and based on student outcomes; this component is typically tied to test scores. Collecting data is not a problem for effective online programs, but deciding what data will be used for the evaluation process is a major decision.

Standards-based frameworks for traditional classroom teachers generally include sections that simply do not apply to online teachers, such as planning and developing lessons and the physical aspects of classroom management. In many online settings, teachers have minimal involvement in curriculum development. Attempting to make this type of evaluation instrument apply to online teaching is like forcing a square peg into a round hole and may even have negative consequences for the online teacher. Online teachers should be evaluated based on how well they meet the expectations of the online program and should not be penalized by an evaluation instrument that does not allow for variances for specialized teachers.

EXPECTATIONS FOR ONLINE TEACHERS

Expectations for online teachers should be jointly developed by a committee of stakeholders that includes online teachers and administrators. The final product will likely include many expectations from the classroom teacher evaluation instrument but should also include criteria specific to the parameters of the online program. In general, an online teacher should possess strong technical skills, the ability to communicate effectively online, and comprehensive content knowledge. Online teaching standards should also encompass expectations for attendance, rates of interaction, and timeliness.

The development of teaching standards and an evaluation process in the Mesa Distance Learning Program (MDLP) can be used as a case study for establishing procedures in other online programs. MDLP did not have written standards for several years after the inception of the program, although the program administrator and specialist did have expectations of teachers. Teachers were part time, with most working online in addition to a full-time assignment at a traditional school, and were formally evaluated by their campus administrator. As the program grew, it became clear that written expectations and a formal online teaching evaluation framework were needed.

The lack of written standards led to problems caused by a misinterpretation of the expectations—particularly the expectations for logging in and response time. A committee composed of administrators and online teachers started by developing standards for teacher behaviors that could be quantified: log-in requirements, response time to student messages, turnaround time for grading, and rate of feedback. The chart below shows the expectations that were developed, along with a scoring system that allows individual teachers to quickly determine if there are any areas for improvement.

Data for individual teachers is collected automatically by the learning management system (LMS) and can be viewed at any time by teachers and administrators. Individual teachers have access to their own data, but administrators and specialists can see data for the teachers they supervise. Individual teacher data is displayed in the following manner:

1. Prompt message box replies—Meets Standard.
2. Message box replies within twenty-four hours—Exceeds Standard.
3. Prompt assignments graded within forty-eight hours—Exceeds Standard.
4. Assignment feedback provided—Exceeds Standard.

		Approaches	Meets	Exceeds
Prompt messagebox replies	average less or equal to...	12 hrs	10 hrs	5 hrs
Messagebox replies within 24 hours	greater or equal to...	80%	90%	100%
Prompt assignment grading	average less or equal to....	36 hrs	24 hrs	15 hrs
Assignment grading within 48 hours	greater or equal to...	85%	90%	95%
Assignment feedback provided	greater or equal to...	85%	90%	95%

Figure 6.1.
Source: Included with permission of the Mesa Public Schools.

This sample indicates that this particular teacher meets the expectations of the online program. The MDLP nomenclature for viewing teacher data on expectations is the standards check.

Since standards check data is continuously collected and available, appropriate checkpoints for teacher performance had to be determined. MDLP decided that teacher data would be collected in monthly cycles, giving teachers the opportunity to "start over" each month. Because the data pool is reset at the beginning of each month, averages are not very accurate during the first week of the month. It was determined that the content specialist and director would review the standards check for each teacher on the last business day of each month. Specific feedback is provided by content specialists to teachers under their supervision, and notations regarding individual teacher performance are entered into the database.

It is important for teachers to be aware of the consequences that will follow if expectations are not met. The rubric shown below outlines the consequences applied when teachers fall behind on one or more of the MDLP teaching standards. The numbers in the first row apply to either the month or number of standards. For example, if a teacher does not meet the expectations for one standard and/or it is the first occurrence of this behavior, the consequences in Column 1 are applied. If a teacher does not meet the expectations for two standards, or fails to meet the standard(s) for two consecutive months, the consequences in Column 2 are applied, and so on. Unexpected situations, such as family emergencies or illness, may prevent a teacher from meeting the MDLP teaching standards during a given month; thus, consequences for fail-

Month/ Standard	1	2	3	4
Logical Consequences	√ Specialist contacts teacher (optional) √ Teacher self-corrects √ Specialist documents actions	√ Specialist contacts teacher √ Specialist documents actions √ Goal-setting √ Teacher must commit to improvement √ Warning: Sections closed if no sign of improvement/possible change in method of pay	√ Specialist contacts teacher √ Specialist documents actions √ Goal-setting √ Teacher must commit to improvement √ Sections closed/change in method of pay	√ Specialist contacts teacher √ Specialist documents actions √ Specialist contacts Director with copy of documented actions √ Students transferred to another teacher √ Meeting with Director regarding future status with program

Figure 6.2.
Source: Included with permission of the Mesa Public Schools.

ing to meet the standards are structured in a manner to allow leniency in these cases. However, MDLP teachers are encouraged to contact the content specialist for substitute coverage until the teacher is able to resume normal duties.

FEEDBACK IS IMPORTANT

The MDLP standards check addressed the mechanics of online teaching, such as logging in regularly and responding to students in a timely manner. However, there are elements of online teaching that cannot be quantified, such as communication skills and the quality of feedback. "Decades of education research support the idea that by teaching less and providing more feedback, we can produce greater learning," says author/consultant Grant Wiggins.[2] Since quality feedback is so critical to the learning process, the MDLP teaching standards had to clearly define the expectations for this component. The MDLP interface allows teachers to provide feedback through the course-specific message box, directly on the assignment, or using both methods. The MDLP LMS tracks the type and amount of feedback provided by individual teachers, and content specialists verify the quality using a random sampling of feedback. Data collected regarding the quantity and method of delivery for feedback is always available in a scattergram format for review by administrators, specialists, and teachers.

On the scattergram, a green dot represents the individual teacher, the blue dots represent all other teachers in a content area or department, and the red dots represent all other teachers in the program. The X axis measures feedback provided directly on the assignment, and the Y axis measures feedback provided through the message box. The feedback standard is met if the teacher's green dot is in the upper half of the scattergram, as shown in Chart 2. Dots in the bottom-left quartile indicate teachers who do not meet the feedback standard, as shown in Chart 1.

The complete evaluation system was presented to the full MDLP teaching staff at an annual staff meeting. Data was collected for the month preceding the meeting, and the initial results were used to demonstrate how the system functioned. One month after informing the teachers about this electronic evaluation system, the evaluation

Scattergram chart 1	Scattergram chart 2
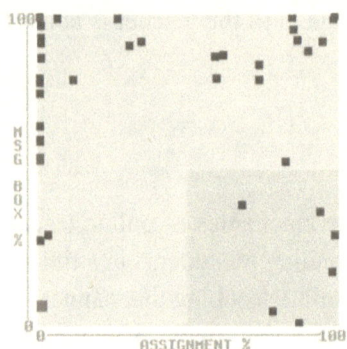	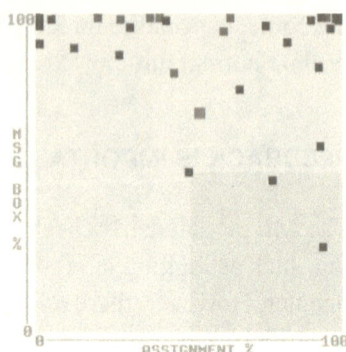

Figure 6.3.
Source: Included with permission of the Mesa Public Schools.

committee took a second look at the data. It appeared that sharing data with the teachers had a positive impact on their teaching behaviors, as illustrated by the scattergram charts. Chart 1 shows the initial snapshot presented to teachers, and Chart 2, created just one month after the staff meeting, shows substantial growth in terms of feedback.

CAN FEEDBACK CHANGE ONLINE TEACHER BEHAVIOR?

The dramatic change in teacher behavior in such a short time prompted investigation into the value of using data sharing as a tool to modify teacher behavior. Doug Barnard and Terry Hutchins conducted a study aimed at addressing this issue, and the purpose of the study is clearly defined in this excerpt:

> To determine if the process used was statistically significant, we took, for each expectation, the first score provided at the fall meeting as our beginning point (Pretest). We then took the score one year later (Posttest) to determine whether or not the gains in teacher performances were significant or not using a simple (t) test of significance. Although most of our teachers were meeting our expectations from day one, we were especially concerned about the few who were doing only enough to get by, but not really putting forth their best effort.[3]

The charts below summarize the findings of the study.

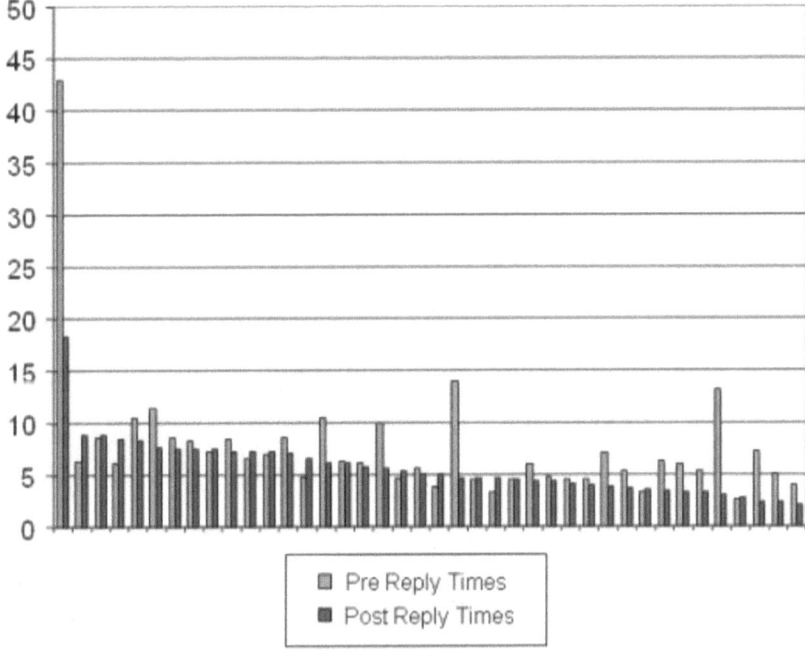

Figure 6.4.

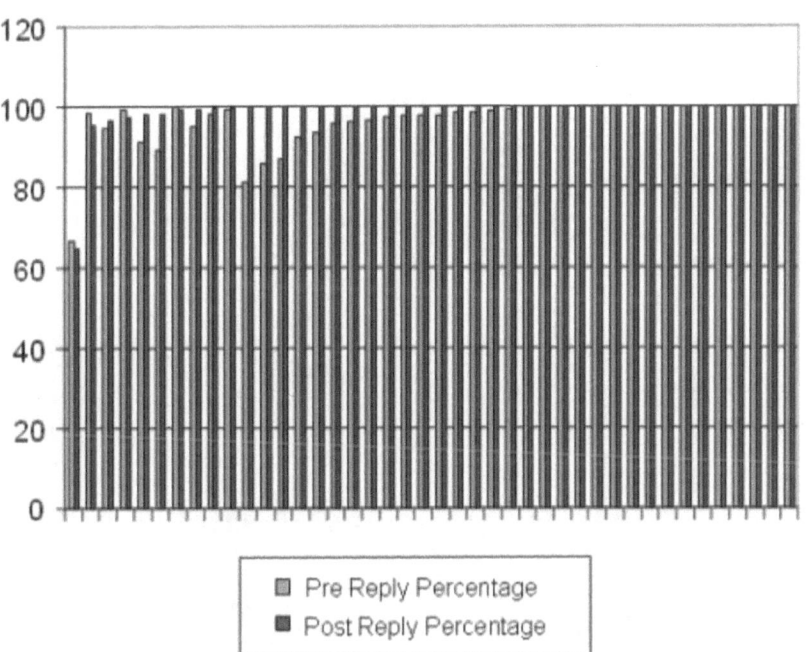

Figure 6.5.

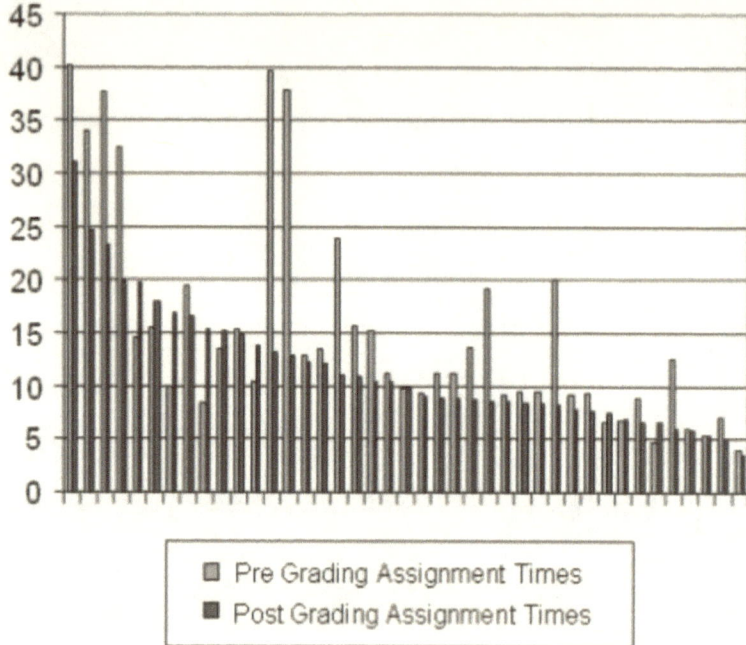

Figure 6.6.

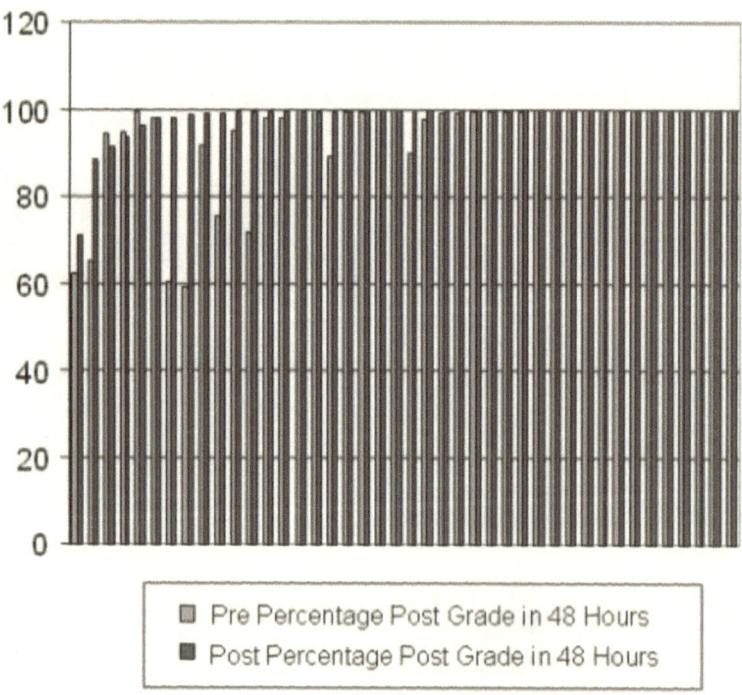

Figure 6.7.

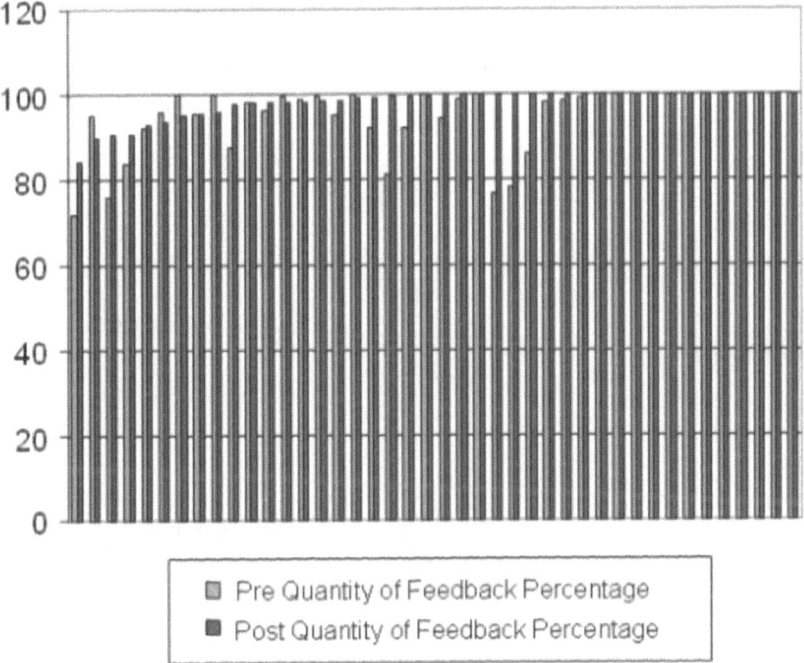

Figure 6.8.

The response times and quality of responses improved from pretest to posttest on all five measures. Teachers responded more quickly after the intervention, and the quality of their feedback improved as well. Of course, those teachers doing a solid job from day one continued on that path for the year. By analyzing the data for just those not meeting expectations on day one, there was a significant difference in their score gains from pretest to posttest. The results of this study revealed that teacher performance was statistically changed for online teachers by providing a list of the expectations, feedback as to how each teacher scored on those expectations, and specific consequences.[4]

Although it was determined that sharing data with teachers motivated them to maintain appropriate teaching behaviors or "self-correct" as needed, MDLP administrators and specialists also believed in the value of having regular conversations with teachers regarding areas of strength and areas for improvement. The focus of these conversations is the quality and efficacy of feedback provided to students. Teachers

Table 6.1. MDLP Content Specialist Evaluation Rubric

Curriculum Specialist

	Ineffective	*Developing*	*Effective*	*Highly Effective*
Produces high-quality courses	Makes content errors when designing curriculum	Includes most important concepts when designing curriculum	Displays solid knowledge of the important concepts when designing curriculum	Applies extensive content knowledge to design curriculum that engages students in significant learning
Demonstrates deep understanding of teaching methods	Lacks knowledge of appropriate strategies for online learning	Is aware of appropriate strategies for online courses: backward design, blended learning, problem-based learning	Is conversant about appropriate strategies for online courses: backward design, blended learning, problem-based learning	Is knowledgeable about and can apply appropriate strategies for online courses: backward design, blended learning, problem-based learning
Participates in program improvement	Resistant to implementation of new ideas	Is open to new ideas, but does not make significant contributions to program development	Key player in development of new programs	Suggests new ideas and is key player in development of new programs

Maintains alignment to changing standards	Does not keep courses updated to align to state and district standards	Becomes aware of changes in standards after the fact, moves slowly to implement changes	Is notified of changes in standards by attending district department meetings, updates courses in reasonable time period	Stays abreast of changes in state and district curriculum and moves quickly to update courses
Displays skill at using software applications	Lack of skill using one or more essential applications (Windows, Microsoft Office, Dreamweaver, Fireworks)	Demonstrates basic skill using essential applications (Windows, Microsoft Office, Dreamweaver, Fireworks)	Proficient at using essential applications (Windows, Microsoft Office, Dreamweaver, Fireworks)	Expertise using essential applications and willingness to learn new programs as needed
Directs own workload	Resistant to guidance to prioritize and organize; lack of organization leads to a failure to meet deadlines	Needs guidance prioritizing and organizing tasks, may struggle to meet deadlines	With guidance prioritizing tasks, can organize workload to meet deadlines while working with frequent interruptions and minimal supervision	Organizes and prioritizes tasks to meet deadlines while working with frequent interruptions and minimal supervision
Responds to feedback for course improvement	Resistant to making course improvements based on feedback	Makes course improvements when provided with suggestions	When provided an analysis of data collected from student, parent, teacher, and partner district comments, can use it to make appropriate course improvements	Conducts analysis of data collected from student, parent, teacher, and partner district comments and uses it to make appropriate course improvements

Table 6.1. *(Continued)*

	Instructional Support			
	Ineffective	*Developing*	*Effective*	*Highly Effective*
Conducts training sessions	Does not conduct effective training for new teachers; does not provide ongoing professional development	Conducts effective face-to-face training sessions for new teachers but fails to provide ongoing professional development	Conducts effective face-to-face training sessions for new teachers; provides additional training upon request	Conducts effective face-to-face training sessions for new teachers; anticipates and provides professional development as needed
Maintains respectful relationships with teachers	Relationships with teachers are not respectful; specialist is not a source of support for teachers	Maintains respectful relationships with teachers, but teacher may not feel comfortable bringing problems to specialist	Maintains highly respectful relationships with teachers	Maintains highly respectful relationships with teachers; teachers feel comfortable seeking out the specialist for support
Provides material support to teachers	Does not offer material support to teachers	Supports teachers by setting up laptops but may not provide ongoing maintenance	Supports teachers by setting up and assisting with the maintenance of laptops	Supports teachers by setting up and assisting with the maintenance of laptops and helping teachers become self-sufficient users

Balances course loads	Does not consider teacher needs or wants when balancing course loads	Attempts to balance course loads	Maintains appropriate student count based on individual teacher's needs	Is proactive in anticipating fluctuations in desired student counts; helps maintain appropriate course loads
Serves as instructional coach	Unable to identify areas for improvement or suggest alternative methods	Wants to help teachers improve, but needs assistance with improvement process	When directed, works with teachers to increase efficiency and efficacy	Proactive in conducting analysis of current methods to help teachers be effective and efficient; suggests alternative techniques
Ensures adherence to MDLP teacher standards	Does not monitor teacher standards and payroll	Monitors teacher standards and payroll, but does not follow up with teachers and/or document conversations	Proactive in monitoring teacher standards and payroll; documents conversations with teachers regarding areas for improvement	Proactive in monitoring teacher standards and payroll; documents conversations with teachers regarding areas for improvement; conversations are effective and lead to improvement

(continued)

Table 6.1. (Continued)

	Peer Relations			
	Ineffective	Developing	Effective	Highly Effective
Conducts professional interactions with all staff members	Communication style can be disrespectful	Adheres to established norms of mutual respect	Open to constructive criticism; conducts relations in a manner that encourages dialogue; adheres to established norms of mutual respect	Open to constructive criticism; shows sensitivity to opposing perspectives and works to build consensus; exercises control in contentious situations
Serves as effective team member	Does not contribute to program goals	Contributes to program goals	Makes significant contributions to program goals	Key player in creating, developing, and contributing to program goals, even those not directly related to content area
Reacts favorably to change	Resistant to changes in procedures and policies	May demonstrate reluctance when faced with changes in policies and procedures	Supports changes in procedures and policies in a professional manner, even when not in full agreement	Identifies when changes in procedures and policies are needed; supports changes in a professional manner, even when not in full agreement
Uses effective communication skills	Written and/or verbal skills do not meet professional standards; fails to maintain confidentiality	Communicates intent in writing and speaking, but skills lack polish; maintains confidentiality	Able to communicate effectively (verbal and written); maintains confidentiality	Superior written and verbal communication skills; maintains confidentiality

Customer Service

	Ineffective	Developing	Effective	Highly Effective
Conducts professional interactions	Lack of positive or respectful demeanor when working with students and parents, district personnel, partner district staff, and the general public	Attempts to maintain a positive and respectful demeanor when working with students and parents, district personnel, partner district staff, and the general public; may lose composure in stressful situations	Maintains positive and respectful demeanor when working with students and parents, district personnel, partner district staff, and the general public	Maintains positive and respectful demeanor when working with others; keeps composure and demonstrates patience in stressful situations; attitude and actions convey desire to be helpful
Solution-oriented attitude	Lack of understanding and/or empathy for problems of students, parents, and partners; does not work toward a solution	Demonstrates understanding of and empathy for problems of students, parents, and partners	Demonstrates understanding of and empathy for problems of students, parents, and partners, and actively seeks solutions to these problems	Demonstrates understanding of and empathy for problems of students, parents, and partners, and actively seeks solutions to these problems; able to resolve issues without elevation
Effective technical support troubleshooter	Is unable to suggest more than one solution to a problem and/or provides inaccurate information	May not be able to help with all problems; may provide inaccurate information on occasion	Attempts multiple solutions to a problem; provides accurate information	Sticks with the customer until all options are exhausted; provides accurate information
Provides timely and accurate responses to questions and concerns	Responses to questions and concerns are not timely and/or accurate	Inconsistent in providing timely and/or accurate responses to questions and concerns	Provides timely and accurate responses to questions and concerns in accordance with MDLP standards	Exceeds expectations for response time and accuracy according to MDLP standards
Corrects technical or content problems in a timely manner	Responses to technical and/or content problems are not timely	Inconsistent in providing timely responses to technical and/or content problems	Provides timely responses to technical and/or content problems	Exceeds expectations for response time to technical and/or content problems

Source: Included with permission of the Mesa Public Schools.

who are not meeting one or more of the MDLP teaching expectations are required to meet with the content specialist to determine ways to assist the teacher in meeting these agreed-upon expectations. Ongoing professional growth is a priority for MDLP, as all teachers—even those who are highly effective—have areas in which it is possible to improve. Regular teacher-specialist conversations are an important strategy to ensure continued teacher development.

EVALUATION OF PROGRAM SPECIALISTS

Content specialists play a critical role in the Mesa Distance Learning Program by developing curriculum and supervising the teachers within their content area. The job duties of a content specialist for an online program are unlike the job responsibilities for other content specialists in a school district, but district policy often mandates that the same evaluation instrument must be used for all specialists. MDLP attempted to address this concern by adjusting the district specialist evaluation instrument to fit the unique characteristics of the MDLP content specialist. MDLP believes it is important for the evaluation instrument to be an accurate reflection of the specialists' day-to-day job responsibilities, so the modified rubric was presented to the district human relations department for consideration. The rubric is shown in Table 6.1 as an example of how existing district evaluation instruments can be modified to meet the particular needs of an online program.

SUMMARY

Schools evaluate teachers for accountability, to ensure quality teaching, and to promote professional development. It is critical for online programs to clarify expectations for teachers and specialists so they can align their behaviors with the desired goals. Making data consistently available for teacher review, providing opportunities to reflect on the data, and conducting regular professional conversations regarding the data will guide administrators, specialists, and teachers along a path of continued growth.

NOTES

1. John P. Papay, "Refocusing the Debate: Assessing the Purposes and Tools of Teacher Evaluation," *Harvard Educational Review* 82, no. 1 (2012): 123.

2. Grant Wiggins, "Seven Keys to Effective Feedback," *Educational Leadership* 70, no. 1 (September 2012), http://www.ascd.org/publications/educational-leadership/sept12/vol70/num01/Seven-Keys-to-Effective-Feedback.aspx.

3. Doug Barnard and Terry Hutchins, "Enhancing Teacher Performance with Online Programs," *Distance Learning Journal* 7, no. 3 (2010): 26–30.

4. Ibid., 9.

CHAPTER 7

Technology, Monitoring, and Functions

The core of an online program is the learning management system (LMS). It allows programs to deliver course content and perform various functions while constantly collecting data regarding student attendance and achievement, teacher activity, and program costs. A top-tier LMS delivers courses and monitors various functions to ensure the system operates smoothly and at a reasonable cost. The integration of course delivery and monitoring allows schools to offer quality, rigorous courses with accountability and credibility. The data collected behind the scenes of a course is critical to the implementation of an improvement ethic in all areas: student achievement, program efficiency, and professional growth for teachers.

When the Mesa Distance Learning Program (MDLP) started in 1999, online learning at the K–12 level was in its infancy, and most commercial learning management systems were designed for higher education. The choices for K–12 schools were few and very expensive. Today, buyers can choose from many learning management systems that offer a variety of options and vary in cost. Making the right choice for a school or program will depend upon budget, the number of students to be served, curriculum, and the level of personnel expertise in the district. The goal is to have a system that allows for basic functions:

1. The course registration process, including a way to handle variances in status, such as part-time and full-time enrollments.
2. Course delivery, including grade-level appropriate instruction that includes interaction with teachers and perhaps other students, as well as assessment.

3. An integrated support system that directs students to and tracks academic and technical support.
4. A method of uploading required data to the state department of education.
5. The capacity to run queries on student and teacher activity.

LMS OPTIONS

The source of the curriculum will be a major driver in the decision-making process when selecting an LMS. There are two choices for a school or program that plans to develop its own course content:

1. Purchase a subscription to an LMS that allows content to be imported.
2. Develop an LMS internally.

There are many good commercial learning management systems that allow content to be imported for use in the K–12 setting. However, there are two major drawbacks of using a commercial LMS: limitations on customization and cost. A commercial LMS will probably not be able to perform all of the monitoring functions required by a school, such as keeping detailed logs that track the activity of students, teachers, and other staff members. Collecting this type of data is important not only because it helps hold students and staff accountable, but also because it is used to identify problems and make improvements. Commercial learning management systems are generally provided at a yearly subscription cost that decreases as the number of seats in the subscription increases, with additional fees for program setup, training, and customization.

The same factors that serve as drawbacks to commercial learning management systems are the reasons a district might choose to develop its own LMS. Although the development of a proprietary management system does require a substantial upfront investment and a continued investment in personnel, the cost is controlled internally and is relatively fixed. The cost savings was noted in the 2007 Arizona Office of the Auditor General's report on K–12 online education: "In contrast, the one school that developed its own learning management system,

Mesa USD, had significant cost savings. . . . Mesa USD's $2,499 per-pupil cost was the second lowest per-pupil cost of all the TAPBI schools."[1]

The benefits of the proprietary LMS developed by MDLP technical staff are not only monetary; having an internally developed LMS provides the program with the flexibility to customize features as needed. For example, none of the commercial learning management systems have the capacity to upload attendance data for K–12 online students to the state. This is a critical flaw; attendance uploads are the way online schools in Arizona are funded. Schools that use a commercial LMS must export data from the LMS into the school information system to be uploaded to the state so funding can be collected. The proprietary MDLP LMS includes a feature that collects student attendance data and allows the data to be uploaded directly to the state department of education.

Schools also have the option of working with a vendor who supplies the LMS, course content, and even the teachers. This is a good option for schools and programs that lack qualified personnel to develop and teach online courses. The obvious downside to this option is cost. When considering a vendor who offers all of these services, be sure to ask the right questions to discover all of the hidden costs before signing on to a subscription.

A final option available to schools interested in starting an online program is to partner with a reputable school district that has an established program. Partnering with an established district provider allows schools to benefit from the wisdom of practitioners who have lived through the development process. This type of partnership allows schools to launch an online program in a relatively short time frame with access to mentors who can offer advice on procedures, staffing, budget, and equipment needs. Districts that want to eventually launch their own program can use the partnership as a learning experience.

MDLP, one of the original K–12 online providers in Arizona, entered into many intergovernmental agreements to help other districts in the state launch their own online programs. MDLP provides its district partners with a customized website, access to the LMS, quality courses built on state standards, and highly qualified teachers. Partner districts also have the option of customizing course content and using their own teachers. Partnering with MDLP is an attractive option for many reasons, including its reputation for offering quality, rigorous courses and being an online provider with integrity. MDLP is also an affordable option for school districts; unlike commercial, for-profit programs, the Mesa Unified School District was not involved in online learning to make money. Partnering with an established district is a reasonable way for a school district to enter the online game by providing students access to quality courses and administrative members access to expertise from a reputable provider, all while protecting districts from any financial risk.

Some vendors in the online arena offer great products in terms of curriculum or learning management systems. However, the bottom line is that commercial programs operate to make a profit, and when the profit margin becomes too slim, companies leave the market. That happened in Arizona. One school district formed a partnership with a commercial online program that claimed it could make money for the school district. Representatives of the company canvased the population centers around the state, seeking student enrollment. When the school district failed to enroll enough students quickly enough to make a profit for the company, the company closed operations in Arizona. Since the commercial program owned everything—course content, servers, LMS—students and the school district were left without an online program midyear. School districts that enter into partnerships with commercial providers operate at the mercy of the commercial provider.

MONITORING EXPECTATIONS

In any school, there are formal and informal standards and expectations for the behavior of faculty and staff. In successful schools and online programs, the most important expectations are clearly defined in writing and closely monitored by the administration. Monitoring clear expectations allows the school leadership to identify areas for improvement. Online schools and programs must work hard to earn a reputation as effective educational institutions, making these procedures even more important.

The Importance of Data

Gathering data allows program administrators to compare reality against expectations. An important—but not always reliable—form of data is anecdotal information from faculty and staff, parents, and students. Consider the following examples of anecdotal information received by an online program administrator related to expectations:

- A content specialist who supervises the English department is frustrated with a teacher who fails to respond to e-mails in a timely manner. As the content specialist considers the situation, she thinks of other incidents in which teachers have not responded quickly to e-mails, causing her to generalize that all of the online teachers are failing to respond to e-mails in a timely manner.
- A parent calls to complain that a final exam for a course did not test the stated objectives.
- A parent visits the office and requests that his child not be placed in a particular math teacher's course, because he has heard from other parents that the teacher is too harsh and demanding of high school students.

Anecdotal information of this nature may or may not be accurate, and so it is important for the program administrator to delay action until further investigation reveals how critical the concern is in reality. A director can make great strides in improving a program by paying attention to the concerns of stakeholders and making note of potential issues. An effective director resolves issues before they become problems; to do that, data is needed.

The nature of online education lends itself to data collection. After defining formal expectations, electronic processes should be devised for monitoring adherence to those processes. Establishing expectations, monitoring the expectations, and responding to the data are the keys to having an improvement ethic. Using data as evidence is the most powerful and effective tool in the improvement process.

Monitoring processes and data collection should be done through the backbone of the online program—the LMS. That is why it is important to identify the program's vision, mission, core beliefs, and expectations before selecting an LMS. It is critical to ensure that the LMS selected for the program is capable of providing the data needed to maintain the improvement ethic. The following list includes examples of processes that should be monitored through the LMS.

1. *Monitoring part-time teacher cost*: Many online programs hire teachers to work on a part-time basis from a remote location. MDLP uses this staffing model, with most teachers working in a full-time capacity at another Mesa Unified School District school while working for MDLP in the evenings and on weekends. For several years, these part-time teachers self-reported the hours they worked for payroll purposes. As the program grew, the question of accountability was raised: how could it be assured that the hours reported were accurate? It was recognized that teachers grading lessons at home could easily be interrupted; a teacher sitting down at the computer to work might be distracted by a child needing help with homework, a telephone call, or many other disruptions. Although the teacher sat at the computer for two hours, how much of that time was actually spent on task? The recording of accurate hours worked is a bit of guesswork.

   The LMS should keep data that allows teachers to be paid for the hours they actually worked. The MDLP LMS tracks the time teachers are logged into their accounts and actively working, and displays the data on the teacher's main screen. In addition, teachers are encouraged to individually track the time spent working so they can compare it to the time tracked by the LMS. This allows teachers to be compensated for time they may work offline. When this system was first implemented, the data revealed that most MDLP teachers were either overpaid or underpaid.

   When it became apparent that teachers were being paid inaccurately, the MDLP leadership team decided to display payroll data in a visual manner for review by individual teachers and program leadership. The payroll chart shows the teacher and his or her student caseload, along with the hours worked as tracked by the LMS and the hours reported to payroll by the teacher. The payroll chart is color-coded to provide a quick visual cue that the hours reported were lower than anticipated (shown in yellow), on target (shown in green), or higher than anticipated (shown in red), and allows program leadership to address any areas of concern.

	--- 21 --- 03/30-04/12				--- 22 --- 04/13-04/26				--- 23 --- 04/27-05/10		
142	13	9	11	99	13	9	13	94	14	8	12
138	24	18	32	128	30	22	40	99	38	44	56
228	23	23	22	186	27	29	26	106	33	35	35
164	33	31	34	130	33	32	34	85	30	28	30
147	24	22	26	130	26	22	27	73	38	33	40
91	17	9	12	79	13	8	11	63	21	9	13
112	22	17	24	110	21	19	24	71	28	22	28
147	22	15	19	150	22	17	21	115	32	28	33
83	8	10	14	72	15	9	14	61	35	12	20

Figure 7.1.
Source: Included with permission of the Mesa Public Schools.

2. *Monitoring academic dishonesty*: The LMS should track student completion of the academic integrity module and any instances of academic misconduct (see Chapter 5 for more details). This data should be included in individual student records that can be accessed as needed by the appropriate personnel.
3. *Monitoring online teachers*: The LMS should collect data used for teacher evaluation (see Chapter 6 for more details).
4. *Final exams and other assessments*: The LMS should perform multiple functions related to assessment, including the scheduling of final exams. Appropriate staff members should be able to adjust testing circumstances as needed, such as turning off the test timer or restricting access to assessments to specific locations.
5. *Technical support*: The LMS should collect data regarding technical support, such as the type of help needed, which member of the staff handled the support request, and how the problem was resolved. Technical support data is highly useful in determining how the structure of the program and user interface can be improved.
6. *Course feedback from students*: Every course should include a course evaluation for students to complete anonymously before taking the final exam. Results of the course evaluation should

be sent to the teacher of record and the content specialist—after the student's personal information has been removed. The data from these evaluations should be stored so it can be compiled for review on a regular basis by the content specialist and teachers of the course.
7. *Feedback from parents*: Parents should have the opportunity to complete anonymous surveys when their student completes an online course. The parent survey will likely have a different focus than the student survey but will still return valuable information about the program structure and the student's experience in a particular course. Parent survey feedback should be collected and compiled for regular review by the school/program leadership team.
8. *Course statistics*: The LMS should have the capability to produce overall course statistics regarding course completion and grade distribution. Displaying data in a visual format, such as charts or graphs, makes it easy to understand. An example is shown below.

Course statistics can suggest areas of strength or weakness, such as courses that are too difficult or lack rigor. However, course statistics are only a starting point for further investigation.

ar21 (ar21): Digital Photo Studio
Completion Rate (minus no-shows): 100%
Average Time to Complete (days): 75
A:5(62.5%) B:1(12.5%) C:2(25%) Total:8
Cmp:8(21.62%) Enr:17(45.95%) NoS:12(32.43%) Total:37

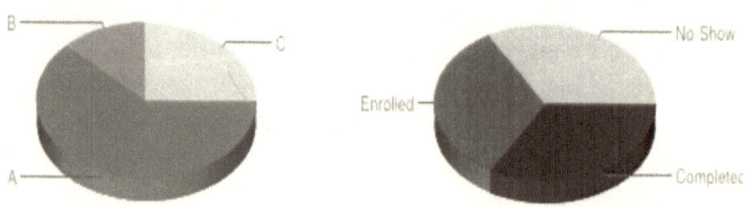

Figure 7.2.
Source: Included with permission of the Mesa Public Schools.

9. *Run queries on demand*: The LMS should allow program administrators to run queries of student, teacher, and staff activity as needed. If the data collected cannot be compiled and accessed on demand, then it is useless.

OTHER FUNCTIONS OF THE LMS

1. *Student Registration System*: The registration process for K–12 students requires input from several sources: students, parents, and school staff. Students and parents provide demographic and personal information, while school counselors or advisers ensure appropriate course selection. The LMS should have the ability to collect input from different sources and combine them into one record in a manner that is simple and easy to use. A sophisticated LMS will have the ability to import data from a school information system, minimizing the amount of information students and parents are required to provide during the registration process.
2. *Access for school staff*: Most enrollments in online programs, particularly at the secondary level, are students who supplement their education at a brick-and-mortar school with one or more online courses, which means that faculty and staff members at schools within a district need access to the online program to monitor student progress. The LMS should allow accounts with different levels of access to be created for school administrators, counselors, and lab teachers. Administrator and counselor accounts should include the ability to approve course selection and monitor student progress, including start and end dates, percentage of course completion to date, and the overall grade. Lab teachers require additional features in their level of access, because they supervise students as they work on classes. It is helpful for lab teachers to be able to view course content, as well as student work and communication with the online teacher.
3. *Student user interface*: Students at the K–12 level work best within a user interface that provides access to all required course features from one log-in screen. After logging in, students should be able to access course content and program announcements

and information, submit course work, and communicate with the teacher of each course. In the early days of online learning, most programs required students to submit assignments via e-mail. Today, most systems embed assignment submission within the course through an assignment dropbox or portfolio, reducing complaints that assignments were submitted but never received by the teacher. The LMS should provide program-level administrators with access to course-specific information (assignments, activity logs, communication with teachers) for all students.

4. *Online help for students and staff:* Effective online programs provide students and staff with online support in the form of FAQs, tutorials, and how-to videos. Common topics addressed for students and parents include configuring the computer for online courses, logging in, contacting the teacher, and submitting assignments. Other support topics for students and parents will be determined by the specific configuration of the program. Online teachers are often working remotely and at odd hours, so it is important for them to have access to an on-demand database of information regarding common technical issues and program procedures.

5. *Accommodating students with individualized education plans (IEPs) and 504 plans*: An essential function of the LMS is to ensure that accommodations for students with IEPs and 504 plans are met, including communication with online teachers and curriculum modifications, such as removing the timer from quizzes and tests.

SUMMARY

Choosing an LMS is one of the most important decisions to be made when starting an online school or program. The functions outlined in this chapter are essential to the success of an online program, whether a commercial LMS is selected or an LMS is developed in-house. Commercial learning management systems allow schools to launch a program immediately, but it is important to determine limitations of the product and any hidden costs upfront. Developing an in-house

LMS allows the program to be personalized to the specific needs of the community and is the most cost-efficient option, but it does require a significant upfront investment and technical expertise. The examples shown in this chapter were pulled from the proprietary system developed by the Mesa Distance Learning Program. It is important to note that this system was not developed overnight; the first iteration was rudimentary, and features were added over the years and continue to be added as needs arise. These examples were included to show how basic functions might work, but the same functions might be accomplished in a different way.

NOTE

1. State of Arizona Office of the Auditor General, *Technology Assisted Project-Based Instruction Program*, 23.

CHAPTER 8

Future Trends and Issues

The best place for most students to learn is in a classroom interacting with the teacher and other students. If this is not possible for whatever reason, then a creditable online program is a reasonable alternative and will continue to be in the future. There is no evidence that online learning will replace the traditional school in the future.[1] However, online learning at the K–12 level will continue to grow as it becomes more integrated into traditional schools.

This chapter will focus on trends and issues in online learning that must be addressed to ensure respect and viability for online programs. These issues surround two key topics:

1. The development and management of online courses.
2. The refinement of statewide policies.

The chapter will close with a recommendation for using online learning in response to school closures caused by pandemics or extreme weather.

DEVELOPMENT AND MANAGEMENT OF ONLINE COURSES

Impact of One-to-One Digital Learning Initiatives

Widespread availability of low-cost yet powerful tablet computing devices has resulted in the foremost trend in education—one-to-one digital learning initiatives. There are lofty goals behind these initiatives: improving student engagement, personalizing learning, providing equitable access to technology, and developing competent and responsible twenty-first-century learners. One-to-one digital learning initiatives have the potential to increase the use of online curriculum throughout schools at all levels but also present a challenge to online programs to develop and deliver content in a format that is accessible on all types of devices.

A quick look at the history of course development in the Mesa Distance Learning Program (MDLP) can be used to illustrate this point. When MDLP started developing its own content, Authorware—a Macromedia product at the time—was the industry standard for developing interactive course content. All of the interactive elements in MDLP courses, including the test engine, were reliant on the Authorware plug-in to function correctly. Macromedia was purchased by Adobe, which eventually ended development and support of the Authorware product. The next big thing in interactive content for the web appeared to be Flash, and so MDLP began shifting interactive content to a Flash format. While this change was under way, Apple announced that Flash would not be allowed on many of its mobile devices, such as iPads. As this book is being written, the MDLP technical staff and content developers are working to create a plug-in-free environment in HTML5 so that content can be accessed on all devices. As school districts move to implement one-to-one digital initiatives, it is important to be cognizant of technology trends to ensure that curriculum is compatible on all devices used by students working on campus and remotely.

Blended Learning

In its earliest days, online learning at the K–12 level was perceived as a threat by many traditional classroom teachers, who worried that teachers would eventually be replaced by computers. Online learning is not a replacement for teachers, but it does change their role. Experience has taught the online community that very few students at the K–12 level are suited to work completely online from home. Even when this is necessary—for students with chronic illness or students who travel, for instance—a teacher is still required to supervise student progress, answer questions, and evaluate student work.

After more than a decade of working in an online environment, the authors of this text believe that the most appropriate use of online courses at the K–12 level is in the form of blended learning. Blended learning can take different forms, as it is applied differently depending upon the school and the learners. However, the use of technology in a classroom alone does not constitute blended learning. Successful blended learning occurs when technology is used thoughtfully to deliver content or create personalized learning experiences to accommodate individual learning styles and needs. A common form of blended learning is "flipping the classroom"—allowing students to access content in the form of text or video in an electronic format, and to participate in discussions, labs, and group activities in the traditional classroom.

The emphasis on blended learning will increase as new examples of effective blended instruction are reported. The increased popularity of integrating technology with curriculum through blended learning is a positive change for schools. Blended learning also allows teachers to fully meet the requirements of the Common Core standards by addressing the discussion, presentation, and speaking components in a face-to-face setting while maintaining personalized learning for individual students.

The challenge for schools will be the effective implementation of blended learning. Chapter 2 addressed the importance of developing a vision before leaping into implementation of an online program, and the same process should apply to the implementation of blended learning. Administrators and teachers should have a clear idea of what issues will be addressed and how learning will be improved through the use of blended learning. Keeping an eye on these targets will determine the appropriate structure for the blended learning program and the technology required for its application.

Open Educational Resources

Open educational resources (OER) are resources that reside in the public domain, allowing for their free use and repurposing by others. OER may include full courses, modules, textbooks, videos, teacher support materials, and other items. According to the Scholarly

Publishing and Academic Resources Coalition: "Open Educational Resources (OER) provide a new model for disseminating knowledge that is designed to take full advantage of the digital environment."[2] Many schools moving toward online and blended learning are tapping into OER to curtail costs and decrease curriculum development time. OER have the potential to improve teaching and learning by providing access to quality content that promotes critical thinking without technical and legal restrictions put in place by commercial vendors and textbook publishing companies.

One caveat applies to the use of OER: because the resources are open, the credentials of the authors are not vetted, and the content has not been reviewed by qualified evaluators. Any OER to be used in a classroom setting, whether it be a traditional, blended, or online setting, should be evaluated for accuracy, quality, and alignment to standards. It is also important to note that some of OER in larger repositories still have some limitations on use, so educators should carefully check copyright information before disseminating or republishing materials.

Competency-Based Learning

According to the U.S. Department of Education, competency-based learning refers to a flexible educational structure that allows students to progress as they demonstrate mastery of academic content, regardless of time, place, or pace of learning. Competency-based strategies include blended and online learning to provide flexibility in the way that credit can be earned or awarded, and provide students with personalized learning opportunities.[3] Proponents of competency-based learning argue that it leads to greater student engagement because the content is tailored to the specific needs of individual students and allows students to work at their own pace.

Competency-based learning holds promise for education because it allows teachers to truly differentiate learning and meet students at their current level. Effective online curriculum affords students the opportunity to move more quickly through content they have mastered and frees up the classroom teacher to focus on large- and small-group activities that emphasize discussion, enrichment, or remediation. In order for competency-based learning to work on a large scale, issues must be addressed: the development of a common definition of mastery in core content areas, the creation of common assessments used to identify mastery, and funding.

High schools award credit based on successful course completion. In a competency-based approach, how will a student be allowed to demonstrate competency that is equivalent to successful course completion? Will one cumulative test serve as evidence of mastery, or will students be required to earn a score of mastery on a series of benchmark assessments? What score constitutes mastery? In addition to questions about how mastery will be demonstrated, questions remain about the quality and rigor of online courses provided by different vendors or programs. Districts and schools moving in the direction of a competency-based approach would be wise to determine the answers to these important questions before selecting a content provider or developing content internally.

In many states, school funding for traditional and online schools is tied to attendance. In a truly competency-based school, it would be possible for an advanced student to earn a high school diploma in fewer than four years, significantly impacting school funding. In some states, state legislatures have addressed the issue by creating new funding models that distribute some funding when the student is initially enrolled and the remaining funds upon successful course completion through demonstrated competency of subject mastery rather than seat time. This type of funding model has the potential to have a negative impact on school funding—especially if a common definition of competency for core courses is not clearly defined.

MDLP uses a competency-based approach in credit recovery courses. In core content courses, students take a pretest at the beginning of each unit. If a score of mastery is earned on the pretest, the student can move on to the next unit. Although it is possible to test out of one or more units, students are still required to pass a comprehensive final exam to earn course credit. This process ensures that the student has significant knowledge before moving on and also gives assurance to the district that students have mastered key concepts, allowing them to be successful at the next level.

STATEWIDE POLICIES

Funding is just one of several key issues in online learning that must be addressed at a state level. Appropriate solutions in four areas will require a collaborative effort from state legislatures, state departments of education, and educators: funding, academic integrity, data collection, and oversight. Online learning at the K–12 level has matured in recent years, but it still has a long way to go to become an integral part of traditional schools. Implementing statewide oversight in these critical areas will improve the quality of online education and provide stability for schools.

Funding

Equitable and appropriate funding models must be developed as competency-based and blended learning initiatives increase in popularity and scope. As mentioned, some state legislatures have attempted to address the problem with models that provide a majority of funding based upon successful course completion. However, online schools and programs regularly make a substantial investment of teacher time and resources in working with students who never successfully complete a course. Funding only for course completion has the potential to make it economically unfeasible for a district or school to maintain an online program, or to cause programs to strictly limit enrollment to high-achieving students.

The other potential negative consequence of this funding model is that it may result in lower standards to ensure all students can successfully complete a course. This is a likely scenario due to the proliferation of private companies in K–12 online learning. In Arizona, certain for-profit online schools are well known to students as places to earn "easy credits"; these programs have lowered the academic level of courses to attract students and siphon funding from district schools. If funding is to be based on successful course completion, then a common definition of what constitutes mastery of core course curriculum must be determined and consistently applied. Students, parents, educational institutions, and employers all deserve an assurance that course completion has prepared the student for the next step, whether that is the subsequent year of a subject at a high school, higher education, or the world of work.

Academic Integrity

The dominance of private corporations in K–12 virtual schooling has also raised concerns about academic integrity, because of the "potential of financial incentives to distort decision making."[4] In order for a program to truly maintain academic integrity, students and faculty alike must obey rules of honest scholarship. This issue was emphasized by the National Education Policy Center at the University of Colorado, Boulder, in a 2011 report: "The obvious answer for conferring legitimacy on students' work in a virtual environment is relatively simple. A trusted organization must administer the most important examinations in person to the individual receiving credit. . . . The lack of face-to-face relationships between students and teachers can lead to abuses that threaten the legitimacy of the entire institution of cyber-schooling."[5] Until all states require vetted proctored environments for all final examinations, and the final exams are determined to be an appropriate measure of mastery, online programs will be viewed as an ineffective option for receiving course credit, resulting in an increased lack of respect for all virtual programs.

Data Collection

Districts and schools are expected to use data-based decision making to guide school improvement. For traditional brick-and-mortar schools, the data to drive decision making exists but is not often used effectively to impact student achievement. Schools have access to data but not in a usable format: "The problem is not a lack of data, says Kathleen Barfield, chief information officer at Edvance Research. 'There's a public perception that schools are swimming in an ocean of data,' she says. 'They may be, but the data isn't in formats or systems that make it easy for them to actually take it out and use it."[6] Schools need help harnessing the flow of data, identifying which data is useful and how to analyze it.

For online schools and programs, the data problem is bigger in scope; state accountability systems lack the ability to attribute individual student data to multiple institutions. Some online programs provide services to students in multiple districts, and the students usually attend a traditional school full time and take one or a few courses online. State accountability systems build school profiles based on test scores but can only attribute data to the school where the student tested. This can be a problem even within a single district, as demonstrated by the Mesa Distance Learning Program. Less than 10 percent of the MDLP student population is composed of full-time students taking only online classes through MDLP, yet the MDLP school label for accountability purposes is created based only on the test scores of the full-time population—because these students tested at the MDLP facility. A large percentage of the students who take courses with MDLP on a part-time basis also attend another Mesa district school, but the state accountability system is incapable of including scores for those students in the data pool used to determine the yearly label.

The flawed state accountability system in Arizona as it applies to online programs has resulted in several negative consequences for the Mesa Distance Learning Program. On the state-mandated annual school report card, MDLP received an inaccurate label and was drawn into a mandatory school improvement process that was time-consuming, lengthy, and not equipped to address the specific needs of online programs. The inaccurate label raised questions among members of the MDLP community, including parents, teachers, and administrators in partner districts, regarding the quality of education delivered to students. The inability of the state to provide student achievement data for all of the students served by MDLP also prevented the leadership team from making data-based decisions about program structure and course design and content.

Incomplete data is a problem faced by online schools and programs in most states. State departments of education must improve data collection and attribution procedures within accountability systems to ensure that online programs are provided with accurate data to make appropriate decisions to increase student achievement.

Oversight of Online Programs

Online programs are here to stay, blemishes and all, even if oversight is lacking. Up to this point, most state departments of education have lacked the will or resources to monitor programs, hold them accountable, and ensure quality. Until there is a system in place to monitor online schools, some of them will continue to function on the fringes. States need to develop minimum standards for online programs and hire independent, knowledgeable experts to develop electronic systems to monitor adherence to these standards.

The need for the measures outlined in this section is illustrated by a recent ruling by the National Collegiate Athletic Association (NCAA): "The National Collegiate Athletic Association (NCAA) won't accept coursework completed by student athletes at two dozen virtual schools operated by K12, Inc., as of 2014–15, at any Division I or Division II college or university."[7] As of this writing, the NCAA had not provided an explanation for its refusal to accept credits from the for-profit program. However, it seems that the greater public, including parents, the military, and institutions of higher education, are catching on to the fact that online education at the K–12 level needs more regulation.

PLANNING FOR SCHOOL CLOSURES

In recent years, the world has witnessed devastation caused by catastrophic storms, and the United Nations and scientists have urged countries to prepare for more serious weather issues in the future. When extreme weather events result in destruction, keeping schools open is not the greatest priority. However, sometimes weather episodes, such as severe cold spells, do not result in destruction but still shut down communities for lengthy periods of time. Communities need a backup system to keep students learning when schools are closed because of weather conditions.

A basic online program would allow students to attend classes remotely from a safe haven where there is shelter and electricity. The program could be provided through the state department of education or on a regional basis, but would require access to quality courses and thoughtful planning. Each state should develop alternative procedures to ensure continuity of instruction in the event of school closures due to extreme weather or pandemics. Successful development of an emergency preparedness plan that uses online learning to ensure continuity of instruction requires knowledgeable personnel at the state level—not a simple task, but attainable with the right leadership.

SUMMARY

In their earliest days, K–12 online programs attempted to recreate the traditional classroom in a virtual format. Today, it is apparent that online curriculum is one of many tools that educators can draw upon to personalize learning, build critical-thinking skills, and engage learners. In fact, online curriculum currently is helping teachers to transform learning within the traditional classroom setting. Leadership is needed from administrators at the state, district, and school levels to provide the vision and oversight to ensure that online learning is used appropriately to arm students with the knowledge and skills needed to be successful in a highly competitive and interconnected world.

NOTES

1. Glass and Welner, "Online K–12 Schooling," 8.
2. Scholarly Publishing and Academic Resources Coalition, "Open Educational Resources," accessed May 1, 2014, http://www.sparc.arl.org/issues/oer.
3. U.S. Department of Education, "Competency-Based or Personalized Learning," accessed May 1, 2014, http://www.ed.gov/oii-news/competency-based-learning-or-personalized-learning.
4. Glass and Welner, "Online K–12 Schooling," 9.
5. Ibid.
6. Dian Schaffhauser, "Swimming with Data," *Journal* (September 12, 2011): 34, accessed May 14, 2014, http://thejournal.com/articles/2011/09/12/swimming-with-data.aspx.
7. Michele Molnar, "NCAA Bans Coursework Completed by Athletes in 24 K12 Inc. Virtual Schools," *Education Week* blog, accessed May 1, 2014, http://blogs.edweek.org/edweek/marketplacek12/2014/04/ncaa_bans_course work_completed_by_athletes_in_24_k12_inc_virtual_schools.html.

Appendix A

Desired Program Attributes

Defining Question	Vision for the Program	Equipment or Space Required	Estimated Cost

1. Who will be served by the program?
   a. Grade levels
   b. Academic levels
   c. Enrollment status			

2. What method of program delivery?
   a. Synchronous
   b. Asynchronous
   c. Blended			

3. Single-district or multi-district program?			

4. Will curriculum be purchased from a vendor or developed in-house?
   a. Vendor
   b. OER
   c. Developed in-house			

5. What LMS will be used?
   a. Closed
   b. Commercial
   c. Open-source
   d. Proprietary			

6. How will communication be maintained among stakeholders?			

7. How many courses will be offered when the program is launched?				
8. Where will students access online courses?				
9. How will the program service students with special needs?				
10. How will the program be hosted?				

11. Who will teach online courses?
   a. Full- or part-time
   b. Payment
   c. Supervision
   c. Training				

12. What other staff will be required to launch the program?				
13. How will student records be managed?				
14. How will the online program be accredited?				
15. How will the program be marketed?				
16. How will technical support be provided to users?				

Bibliography

Barnard, Doug, and Terry Hutchins. "Enhancing Teacher Performance with Online Programs." *Distance Learning Journal* 7, no. 3 (2010).

Bathon, Justin. *Model Legislation Related to Online Learning Opportunities for Students in Public Elementary and Secondary Education Schools*. Boulder, CO: National Education Policy Center, 2011. Accessed April 1, 2014. http://nepc.colorado.edu/publication/online-k-12-schooling.

Bushaw, William J., and Shane J. Lopez. "The 45th Annual PDK/Gallup Poll of the Public's Attitudes Toward the Public Schools." Phi Delta Kappa International, August 21, 2013. http://pdkintl.org/noindex/2013_PDKGallup.pdf.

Council of Chief State School Officers. "Common Core State Standards." Washington, DC: National Governors Association Center for Best Practices, 2010.

Gemin, Butch, Amy Murin, Chris Rapp, John Watson, and Lauren Vashaw. *Keeping Pace with K–12 Online and Blended Learning: An Annual Review of Policy and Practice*. Evergreen Education Group, 2012. http://kpk12.com/cms/wp-content/uploads/KeepingPace2012.pdf.

Glass, Gene V., and Kevin G. Welner. *Online K-12 Schooling in the U.S.: Uncertain Private Ventures in Need of Public Regulation*. Boulder, CO: National Education Policy Center, October 2011. Accessed April 1, 2014. http://nepc.colorado.edu/publication/online-k-12-schooling.

Horn, Michael B. "Is K–12 Blended Learning Disruptive? It Depends." Clayton Christensen Institute for Disruptive Learning (blog). May 2013. http://www.christenseninstitute.org/is-k-12-blended-learning-disruptive-it-depends/.

Hubbard, Burt, and Nancy Mitchell. "Achievement of Online Students Drops over Time, Lags State Averages on Every Indicator." Chalkbeat

Colorado, October 3, 2011. Accessed October 1, 2013. http://co.chalkbeat.org/2011/10/03/achievement-of-online-students-drops-over-time-lags-statewide-averages-on-every-indicator/.

McTighe, Jay, and Grant Wiggins. *Understanding by Design: Professional Development Workbook*. Alexandria, VA: Association for Supervision and Curriculum Development, 2004.

Molnar, Michele. "NCAA Bans Coursework Completed by Athletes in 24 K12 Inc. Virtual Schools." *Education Week* (blog). Accessed May 1, 2014. http://blogs.edweek.org/edweek/marketplacek12/2014/04/ncaa_bans_coursework_completed_by_athletes_in_24_k12_inc_virtual_schools.html.

National Center on Universal Design for Learning. "What Is UDL?" Last modified April 17, 2013. http://www.udlcenter.org/aboutudl/whatisudl.

Office of the Legislative Auditor State of Minnesota. "Evaluation Report K–12 Online Learning." Accessed October 1, 2013. http://www.auditor.leg.state.mn.us/ped/pedrep/k12oll.pdf.

Papay, John P. "Refocusing the Debate: Assessing the Purposes and Tools of Teacher Evaluation." *Harvard Educational Review* 82, no. 1 (2012): 123.

Republican National Committee. "Resolution Concerning Common Core Education Standards." April 12, 2013. http://www.gop.com/wp-content/uploads/2013/07/Resolution_Concerning_Common_Core_Education_Standards.pdf.

Schaffhauser, Dian. "Swimming with Data." *Journal* (September 12, 2011): 34. Accessed May 14, 2014. http://thejournal.com/articles/2011/09/12/swimming-with-data.aspx.

Scholarly Publishing and Academic Resources Coalition. "Open Educational Resources." Accessed May 1, 2014. http://www.sparc.arl.org/issues/oer.

State of Arizona Office of the Auditor General. "Technology Assisted Project-Based Instruction Program: Auditor General Performance Audit Report 4th Follow-Up Report." Accessed October 1, 2013. http://www.azauditor.gov/Reports/School_Districts/Statewide/tapbi/Oct07/TAPBI_4thFollowup.pdf.

U.S. Department of Education. "Competency-Based or Personalized Learning." Accessed May 1, 2014. http://www.ed.gov/oii-news/competency-based-learning-or-personalized-learning.

U.S. Department of Education. "Race to the Top Executive Summary." November 2009. http://www2.ed.gov/programs/racetothetop/executive-summary.pdf.

United States Census Bureau. "The 2012 Statistical Abstract, Education." Elementary and Secondary Education, Schools Enrollment Table 243. Accessed October 9, 2013. https://www.census.gov/compendia/statab/cats/education.html.

United States Federal Law. Higher Education Opportunity Act. Pub. L. No. 107-296 (2008). http://www.gpo.gov/fdsys/pkg/PLAW-110publ315/pdf/PLAW-110publ315.pdf.

Wiggins, Grant. "Seven Keys to Effective Feedback." *Educational Leadership* 70, no. 1 (September 2012). http://www.ascd.org/publications/educational-leadership/sept12/vol70/num01/Seven-Keys-to-Effective-Feedback.aspx.

William and Flora Hewlett Foundation. "Open Educational Resources." Accessed November 11, 2013. http://www.hewlett.org/programs/education-program/open-educational-resources.

About the Authors

Dr. Doug Barnard is the founding executive director of the Mesa Distance Learning Program. This online program of the Mesa Unified School District was one of first online public school programs to be initiated; it is now the largest public school program in Arizona and the second largest in the nation. The *Arizona Republic* has called him "the Dean of Online Programs" in Arizona.

He has been a teacher at the elementary, secondary, and college levels for several years and also served as assistant superintendent of curriculum and instruction for the Mesa Public Schools for sixteen years. He received his BS degree from Arizona State University, his MS degree from the State University of New York, and his doctorate from Boston University.

Dr. Barnard has authored over twenty-five articles, consulted at over thirty school districts, and been a frequent speaker at conventions and conferences. He has also authored three educational books.

Jennifer Echols earned a BA in secondary education and history from Arizona State University, and MEd degrees in educational technology and educational leadership from Northern Arizona University. She taught social studies and computer and technical education classes in a secondary classroom for ten years before joining the Mesa Distance Learning Program as a content specialist, and has continued in that capacity for the past eleven years.

Echols joined MDLP in the infancy of online learning at the K–12 level. Over the years, she has been instrumental in the development of the program structure, proprietary learning management system, and development of curriculum. She has also served as a consultant to other school districts and private institutions as they seek to develop and implement online programs.

www.ingramcontent.com/pod-product-compliance
Lightning Source LLC
Chambersburg PA
CBHW030145240426
43672CB00005B/281